Reaching and Teaching All Children

**CORWIN
PRESS**

The Corwin Press logo—a raven striding across an open book—represents the happy union of courage and learning. We are a professional-level publisher of books and journals for K–12 educators, and we are committed to creating and providing resources that embody these qualities. Corwin's motto is "Success for All Learners."

Reaching and Teaching All Children

Grassroots Efforts That Work

Editors
Robert L. Sinclair
Ward J. Ghory

CORWIN PRESS, INC.
A Sage Publications Company
Thousand Oaks, California

For information:

Corwin Press, Inc.
A Sage Publications Company
2455 Teller Road
Thousand Oaks, California 91320
E-mail: order@corwin.sagepub.com

SAGE Publications Ltd.
6 Bonhill Street
London EC2A 4PU
United Kingdom

SAGE Publications India Pvt. Ltd.
M-32 Market
Greater Kailash I
New Delhi 110 048 India

Printed in the United States of America

Library of Congress Cataloging-in-Publication Data

Main entry under title:

Reaching and teaching all children: grassroots efforts that work /
edited by Robert L. Sinclair and Ward J. Ghory.
   p. cm.
Includes bibliographical references and index.
ISBN 0-8039-6528-1 (cloth: acid-free paper). — ISBN
0-8039-6529-X (pbk.: acid-free paper)
   1. Public schools—United States. 2. Educational equalization—
United States. 3. Educational evaluation—United States.
4. Teaching—United States. 5. Educational change—United States.
I. Sinclair, Robert L. (Robert Leo), 1939-   . II. Ghory, Ward J.
LA217.2.R42 1997
371.01′0973—dc21   97-4787

This book is printed on acid-free paper.

97 98 99 00 01 02 03   10 9 8 7 6 5 4 3 2 1

Editorial Assistant: Kristen L. Gibson
Production Assistant: Denise Santoyo
Cover Designer: Marcia R. Finlayson

Contents

Foreword

As a program officer at the Danforth Foundation, I found great pleasure in seeing what began as a few ideas on a piece of paper evolve into bold actions for change in public schools. The National Coalition for Equality in Learning is a fine example of how creative ideas can lead to such meaningful action. Hence, for me, this foreword is a celebration of 5 years of work with the National Coalition to improve the learning of all children, including those who find themselves in a position of marginality and are not succeeding in school. Those of us involved in this grassroots effort to improve schools and increase learning are drawn together by a sense of urgency. We believe that if we can discover ways to alter the conditions of these children's school experiences we can change the shape of the future for a significant number of young people in this country. This book tells the story of this adventure in school reform.

This reform effort is not about who is in charge, who handles the funds, or who makes the decisions. This work in local schools did not begin by trying to determine how we should change the curriculum or train the teachers. Rather, the focus was on the children and their learning. For me, this was a breath of fresh air. Certainly, issues about curriculum and instruction came up eventually, but they were raised in a context of improving learning. Whatever changes were proposed had to focus on helping children learn more effectively.

As you read this account of school change, you will discern a way of thinking that speaks to the very heart and soul of committed educators. For example, the National Coalition for Equality in Learning considers quality public education to be a moral imperative of a democratic society. Because an educated citizenry is the bedrock of a democracy, nurturing our public schools is essential to a strong and flourishing civil society in the United States.

Another idea advanced is that parents are partners in education. This is a connection that exists whether educators acknowledge it or not. When home and school join in providing conditions that promote learning, academic success becomes a reality and the quality of life improves, even for those individuals who were previously on the margins of school success. This improvement is not short term. Rather, it continues in an atmosphere of trust and respect where people in both settings take seriously their responsibility for helping children improve their learning. Schools and homes together can create conditions for effective learning. Participants in the National Coalition believe that by creating a community for learning in local schools, all children of all families have an equal opportunity to obtain a high-quality education. It is in our schools that the concept of equality can become real to our children—or it can be lost to them.

To emphasize the importance of equality to learning, the National Coalition has created "Equality Schools." These schools are becoming communities for learning where all students see themselves as productive individuals who can benefit from their school experiences. Teachers and students in Equality Schools are constantly searching for ways to use their creative intelligence to identify and solve learning problems. They are encouraged to discover their own strengths and to use these strengths to correct their particular weaknesses. Equality Schools encourage students and teachers alike to take risks without fear of failure. One exciting discovery about Equality Schools is that although each is unique in its organization, all are alike in their participants' desire to find appropriate responses to strengths and weaknesses that children bring to the school situation.

It is a pleasure to watch children succeed and to see teachers use their creative intelligence to meet the varied needs of their students. I enjoy seeing teachers work harder and claim that their burdens have lightened. I take pride when educators rediscover that spark that brought them to teaching in the first place.

The National Coalition for Equality in Learning has created a grassroots effort that works to make local schools places where all children learn well. This book, then, is about solving problems through discovery. It is about living and learning in community. It is about educators and children in this country, in all their diversity, coming together to ensure equality, to appreciate differences, and to celebrate progress in learning. There are no recipes for reform, only challenges for change.

KATHRYN E. NELSON
RETIRED PROGRAM DIRECTOR
THE DANFORTH FOUNDATION

Preface

This book illuminates the efforts of the National Coalition for Equality in Learning to help educators attack compelling problems of inequity that persist in public education. Members of the National Coalition carefully reflect on the results of their effort to renew leadership and strengthen problem solving in local settings so that unsuccessful youngsters are helped to reach high standards of learning. The call for action in this book echoes democratic values that have deep roots in the history and imagination of our country. Simply put, the National Coalition works for greater equality and increased quality in public schools.

The ideas presented here are intended to widen the circles of discussion and seize the agenda for action to make public schools even more effective in preparing all children and youth for thoughtful participation in our democracy. This book reveals a shared commitment to strengthening our society by improving our nation's public schools. From this commitment comes creative thinking and constructive action so that improved learning of youngsters who are often forgotten or ignored is accomplished in schools participating in the National Coalition for Equality in Learning and eventually in schools across the country. The National Coalition's commitment is expressed in its six interrelated objectives:

- Help students improve their learning and increase their academic and personal success in schools
- Identify local priorities that may have national significance for helping students succeed in school
- Discover constructive ways for teachers, students, and parents to work together to help students improve their learning

- Create conditions in school and nonschool settings that are responsive to the learning problems of students
- Establish partnerships among schools, universities, and community agencies to help students improve their learning
- Demonstrate that by helping students improve their learning, individual schools make more effective use of existing resources

Located in Apple Valley, Minnesota; Boulder, Colorado; Montgomery, Alabama; New Orleans, Louisiana; Plymouth Meeting, Pennsylvania; San Francisco, California; Spring, Texas; and Victoria, Texas, the National Coalition for Equality in Learning is completing a 5-year effort to help all children of all families realize their personal and academic promise. With headquarters in the School of Education at the University of Massachusetts (Amherst), the National Coalition is supported with major funding by The Danforth Foundation and Dr. Camille Cosby. Significant contributions from the school districts and the 65 elementary and secondary schools involved also help the National Coalition accomplish its objectives.

These demographically diverse elementary and secondary schools form a national laboratory for important experiments in school improvement. Member schools, selected because of their strong desire to help all students learn well, represent the stubborn economic realities and serious social challenges that confront public education in our society (Ghory, 1992).[1] Because the National Coalition is a microcosm of the pressing problems and varied resources that characterize U.S. education, the progress that is made in these local schools may help others find ways to create conditions for effective learning.

Public schools united by democratic values emphasizing education as a moral imperative, respect for individuals, pragmatic problem solving, and local control are an unusual phenomenon on the landscape of educational reform. In the chapters of this book, these democratic values appear repeatedly, expressed in familiar ways that remind us of the reasons we entered the educational profession. These values are woven through the substance of the chapters describing important developments taking place in the National Coalition for Equality in Learning.

Chapter 1 is centered on the use of democratic values as a starting point for reforming public schools. The responsibility of public schools to help all children of all families learn well is explained.

Chapter 2 furnishes a useful view of leadership that serves as a background for helping children from various circumstances learn effectively. Central to this leadership are moral imperatives that are likely to ensure equality in public schools.

Chapter 3 covers some of the major lessons learned from our efforts to help elementary and secondary schools make desired changes. The lessons reported in this chapter focus attention on reconsidering conventional approaches to educational change.

In Chapter 4, the crucial roles that teachers may play in designing learning conditions that encourage all youngsters to succeed in school are considered. Teachers are viewed as key leaders for identifying stubborn learning problems, inquiring into why they persist, and creating and testing solutions. The authors further suggest that teachers not only have the best information for designing alternative solutions but that they are also in the best position to try them out to see if the solutions work for the children they serve.

Chapter 5 suggests why it is important for teachers and family members to combine energies so that children may learn even better. The purpose here is to blend educational conditions in schools and homes so that children benefit from both places. The author describes an interesting way for teachers to use family stories to find strengths in homes where adverse circumstances prevail.

In Chapter 6, characteristics of Equality Schools are described so that educators may sense the potential that this constructive concept of a school has for reaching and teaching all children of all families.

Chapter 7 provides useful direction for evaluating the learning progress of children. Educators are challenged to see evaluation as a means for improving learning of all students rather than as a way for sorting students and giving only a small portion of the children access to advanced learning. The authors also call for a constructive balance between standard evaluations developed by specialists who are often isolated from educational practice and local evaluations created by teachers who are close to activities and learning in the school.

Finally, Chapter 8 suggests constructive directions for leadership intended to improve local schools and increase learning for all children.

As a quiet effort for improving public schools and increasing student learning, we keep a sharp edge honed by our mutual interest in excellence with decency. This edge persists because of our belief that regardless of who created the problems of inequality that some children experience in public schools, we are all equally responsible for solving them.

Notes

1. National Coalition schools differ in grade level, with 54% elementary schools, 25% middle or junior high schools, and 21% high schools. They come in a variety of sizes: Nearly half (48%) serve 400-799 students, 26% are small (under 400 students), 23% are large (800-1,799 students), and there were three very large schools (over 1,800). Three fourths of the schools served a significant percentage of children from low-income backgrounds (over 20% qualifying for free lunch), and in one fourth of the schools, over 60% of the students qualified for federal assistance. Finally, the National Coalition enlisted schools representing a significantly diverse ethnic mix, undoubtedly a more diverse ethnic mix than the U.S. public school population as a whole. Over one third of the schools had student bodies in which a majority of the students were "students of color." The challenge of creating school environments where children from many ethnic and economic backgrounds succeed in their learning can be faced productively in the National Coalition.

References

Ghory, W. J. (1992, September). *National Coalition for Equality in Learning: Year two evaluation report, 1991-92.* (Available from the Center for Curriculum Studies, University of Massachusetts School of Education, Amherst, MA)

Acknowledgments

The National Coalition for Equality in Learning is indebted to all the teachers, parents, administrators, and community members who are participating in this experiment to help all children improve their learning. We are particularly grateful to the colleagues who invested their creativity and intelligence in the preparation of this timely book about working in local schools to create conditions for effective learning.

The members of the advisory board, Norma Jean Anderson (chairperson), Camille Cosby, Joseph Novello, William Scheel, and Elizabeth Taylor, kept this project moving forward in a constructive and innovative manner. We very much appreciate their thoughtful guidance, often expressed in spirited ways, that made us think carefully and act wisely. As the first chairperson of the advisory board, Ralph Tyler served as mentor for everyone connected with this adventure. His creative way of solving problems, his high standards of excellence, and his gentle concern for others are truly missed.

We are also grateful to the many graduate students who contributed to our efforts. Mohammed Good, David Raker, Jessica Tatlock, and Shuli Xu provided exceptional help in preparing the manuscript. We are particularly appreciative of the careful attention that David and Jessica gave to the editorial improvements of each chapter. The rigorous intellect and kind spirit of the graduate students in the National Coalition for Equality in Learning confirm that we made a wise decision to become educators.

About the Authors

Ward J. Ghory is Director of the Upper School at Buckingham, Browne and Nichols School in Cambridge, Massachusetts, and Evaluator for the National Coalition for Equality in Learning.

Jan Jacob is Associate Superintendent of Curriculum and Instruction for the Victoria Independent School District in Victoria, Texas, and a School District Facilitator for the National Coalition for Equality in Learning.

Stephanie Knight is Professor of Education at Texas A&M University in College Station, Texas, and a member of the National Faculty of the National Coalition for Equality in Learning.

Hope Jensen Leichter is the Elbenwood Professor at the Elbenwood Center for the Study of the Family as Educator at Teachers College, Columbia University, and a member of the National Faculty of the National Coalition for Equality in Learning.

Kathryn E. Nelson is Program Director (retired) for the Danforth Foundation in St. Louis, Missouri, and East Coast Coordinator for the National Coalition for Equality in Learning.

Robert L. Sinclair is Professor of Education at the University of Massachusetts in Amherst, Massachusetts, and Director of the National Coalition for Equality in Learning.

Robert G. Smith is Associate Superintendent of Curriculum and Instruction for the Spring Independent School District in Spring,

Texas, and a School District Facilitator for the National Coalition for Equality in Learning.

Kimberly Trimble is Associate Professor of Teacher Education at California State University, Dominguez Hills, in Carson, California, and West Coast Coordinator for the National Coalition for Equality in Learning.

Robbie Jean Walker is Dean of Liberal Arts at Auburn University in Montgomery, Alabama, and a member of the National Faculty of the National Coalition for Equality in Learning.

Valerie Wheeler is an English teacher at Casey Middle School in Boulder, Colorado, and a member of the National Faculty of the National Coalition for Equality in Learning.

*This book is dedicated to Dr. Camille Cosby, who helps
teenage mothers continue their learning so their children may
also gain access to a high-quality education on equal terms.*

Realizing Our Promise   1

ROBERT L. SINCLAIR
WARD J. GHORY

The promise to educate all children of all families, and to do it well, is as crucial as any democratic principles of the United States. The wonderful faith that every American is capable of the kind of intellectual competence previously attained by only a small minority of learners (for a concise statement of this ideal, see Maier, 1995) stems from the need for an educated citizenry to participate fully in the complex deliberations of a modern democratic society. In the 20th century, universal suffrage was extended to all citizens in the United States, regardless of race, gender, or ethnic heritage, and a free public education was made available for all children through high school. When John Dewey (1916) brought suffrage and education together in an important book early in the century, his insistent message was that a democratic society must provide equal educational opportunity, not only by giving to all of its children a guaranteed number of years in school but also by making sure to provide for them all an equivalent quality of education (see also Adler, 1982). Since then, the public has gradually understood that Dewey's ideal of universal quality education is essential not only to the optimum working of our political institutions but also for the efficiency of our businesses, the vitality of our culture, and the ultimate good of our citizens as individuals. As President Clinton underscores with his 1996 campaign promise to extend free public education through the first 2 years of college, the mission of public schools in the United States is to provide a high-quality education for all children.

Today's school leaders are successful in creating conditions that help a significant portion of young people learn at high levels of accomplishment. Yet, among informed citizens and caring educators, there is mounting dissatisfaction about the many students who fail to learn what the schools are expected to teach. Thoughtful Americans also are troubled by the realization that children who are marginal in their learning and disconnected from the conditions created to help them succeed in school often come from poverty and, disproportionately, from African American, Asian American, Hispanic, and Native American families. There are still children of some families who are not benefiting fully from their school experiences. The ideal Dewey and others set before us is a challenge we are facing squarely yet not meeting fully.

Nor have we always been honest in our commitment to democracy and its promise of equality. A part of our population, and even a portion of our nation's educators, still hold the opinion that many children are not fully educable—that they are unable to shoulder the duties of self-governing citizens, excluded by the limits of their births and the status of their families from participation in the higher life of the human mind and spirit. This insidious hypocrisy implies that democratic citizens are born, not nurtured through education and informed participation in civic and cultural life. To counter the perception that there are unteachable children and to renew the public school as the gateway to equality, we must find ways to reach and teach all children of all families.

Democratic Values and the Reform of Public Schools

In the past 20 years, two major educational trends have reinforced one another—first, a growing willingness to criticize and attack our schools and, second, a "flight from democracy" characterized by deciding solutions to the problems of public schools at great remoteness from the local school and its community (Park & Boyd, 1994). As the media stoked general frustration about the alleged failures of public schools, reformers on both the left and the right called for interventions in public education that repudiated democratic values by moving the locus of decision making for school improvement farther and farther away from the local school. For example, since 1954, reformers have depended on the courts to impose and monitor necessary desegregation solutions. After Ronald Reagan's Department of Education trumpeted the "rising tide of mediocrity" in 1983, the action shifted to the states, which began competency testing and prescribing statewide cures intended to increase academic achievement. Although well intended, these prescriptive solutions were often misguided. Students tell us that the medicine was worse than the disease.

Central offices in school districts mimic these distant solutions to local problems. Too often, for example, the preferred method of intervention by school boards is to adopt a packaged curriculum or preplanned teacher training program and implement it across all schools in the district, regardless of its fit with the specific learning problems being encountered in each school. When this does not work well, some boards flirt with the solution of hiring private corporations to manage public schools. The assumption behind the transfer of power to state agencies or for-profit businesses and away from the local schools is transparently based on criticisms leveled without solid evidence: that teachers and principals either do not care about academic excellence for all students or are helpless to accomplish it. Possibly, teachers and principals hesitate to change for good reason. In the schools where we toil, educators do not want to take a step unless it is in the direction of equality.

This trend to criticize schools and then strip them of the power to transform themselves is contradictory to the goal of extending academic excellence more broadly. We are finding that lasting change cannot be accomplished in a top-down manner, mandated by distant leaders who drop in occasionally from the cumulus clouds to do their dirty laundry. Instead, the values that drive grassroots improvement efforts derive from a desire to work in a way that is consistent with the mission of public schools in a democracy and responsive to the reality that persists in local schools. For public schools to be the workshops where democracy is renewed as a vision for each generation, the efforts to help schools become even more effective must reflect the democratic values desired. We do not think reform policies imposed from a distance by fiat will result in school improvements that make the educational environment more democratic. Nor do we think it is possible for an autocratic school to prepare young people for constructive participation in our democracy. Let us now consider four democratic values that we believe will serve as guides for creating public schools that we find effective in helping all children of all families fulfill their life's potential.

Education as a Moral Imperative

In a democracy, public education is one important vehicle for improving civil society and perpetuating civic culture. As Benjamin Barber (1995) concisely puts it, "If there is to be a common American people pursuing a common American good, there must be common schools"; the founders of the republic and the first promoters of public schools believed that, "without public education, there could be no democratic public" (p. 34). Schools in a democracy are designed to prepare leaders who will improve society, as well as individuals who will hold the leaders accountable. So, the first moral imperative for education is to perpetuate democratic society as a continuously self-correcting system.

Because educators are entrusted with the young, another moral imperative is to help each generation live in safe, constructive, and healthy ways. In a postmodern world in which parenting itself is at risk, schools increasingly become custodians of the spirits, as well as the minds, of our children. The complete development of individuals—intellectually, emotionally, socially, physically, morally, aesthetically—is a charge gradually assigned to educators, in partnership with parents and guardians. This custodial responsibility is added as a response to a growing recognition that so many students come to school "with shattered dignity, and frightened selves, and a hurt too deep for human eyes to tolerate" (Walker, 1996). As public schools did with many immigrants in the early 20th century, they now again must provide sanctuaries where all the young have a chance to excel in spite of social odds.

Attention to these and other educational imperatives lends a moral urgency to the work of educators. More than in many professions, educators enter their workplaces with bright hopes in the power of their leadership to transform individual lives and shape society. Too often in a climate of hostility to public schools, the reasons teachers enter their profession become fleeting memories, replaced by mindless routines and demeaning responsibilities that chip away at the authority professionals must bring lightly to weighty decisions. To carry on their work in an inspiring manner, educators must return repeatedly to their sense of mission, tapping "that bright reservoir from which hope and joy and aspiration spring" (Walker, 1996). Public school reform movements, born primarily from sharp criticisms of current efforts to help children learn, miss the added dimension of inspiration even as they burden teachers and principals with a haunting view of failure and a lingering sense of feeling unappreciated by the society educators once dedicated themselves to serve. Men and women working with the young in schools need vision more than criticism to sustain them. They must believe that there is purpose and possibility in their work if they are to find the energy to persevere and the creativity to help all children learn well. Fresh urgency and persistent energy may be found by continually viewing the work of school improvement in the light of the mission of public schools in a democracy.

Respect for Individuals

The second democratic value that animates our work is an abiding respect for individuals. The founders of the United States were acutely conscious of the limitations that an inequitable colonizing power imposed on their freedom. They crafted the political checks and balances enshrined in our Constitution as an antidote to prevent the U.S. government from ever reproducing the constraining powers of King, Parliament, and Church. To do so, they explored and expanded their conception of proud individuals with inalienable rights, for whom opportunities to develop and prosper must be preserved at all costs. As Dewey (1916) notes, their positive ideal was humanity, liberated through education to participate in an abundant natural environment and a democratic state. Universal public education became "the first step to free individuals from external chains by emancipating them from the internal chains of false beliefs and ideals" (p. 92). To the heralds of this gospel, all children, youth, and adults (ultimately women and men of all races, classes, and religions) were perfectible individuals whose capacities could be expanded in a progressive society.

Educators are evoking the positive promises of the United States when they propose as the criterion for educational excellence the success of all children and call upon public schools to not only celebrate but look beyond the accomplishments of those at the academic top to consider as well the progress of those forgotten in the middle or languishing on the margins. The insistence that we educate all children of all families draws our attention to the growing diversity of our society, demanding that we not subtly lower our expectations for children from any group or any family configuration. Indeed, the call that we educate all youngsters on equal terms makes us elevate our aspirations across the board, so that no less is expected from other people's children than that which we encourage in our own. Along with an expanded view of excellence as a goal for all of our children comes renewed leadership for the task of creating school environments where each child learns well.

This consideration for individuals that is grounded in our democratic landscape requires us to expand our horizon of what is valuable in children. Just as we recognize the right of all citizens to stand up and speak at town meetings because their insight or comment might be the one that makes clear the problem at hand, so too in our classrooms must teachers tap the intelligence and develop the talent our diverse population possesses. We must identify and build on student strengths if students are to give us their best. In the end, respect for individuals is the path to success for all.

Pragmatic Problem Solving

Americans are famous for a pragmatic, can-do attitude. We instinctively ask, "What works?" Impatient with cant, we want our theories to prove out in practice. So, when our ideology celebrating an education for all on equal terms falters on the reality of some students having difficulty learning in school, we seek straightforward solutions.

Our work together teaches us that when a youngster is having trouble learning, it is necessary to study that student and the conditions that seriously affect his or her learning. Some of these crucial conditions are inside the individual while others are external to the student. Labeling students as "learning disabled," "at risk," or "disadvantaged" because of a few symptoms of their problem is short-sighted and not productive. Rather, it is necessary to look intensively at the conditions that block effective learning and to act directly to create more conducive environments for learning. Our findings show there is no one way to solve learning problems. Rather, improvement is likely to result when educators understand the student as a unique person with assets as well as limitations and when they see the learning environment in a clear-sighted way as a complex of intellectual, social, and physical conditions that might favor or restrict the learning opportunities for this individual. In a pragmatic way, educators participating in our work believe that the more we understand the learning problem and why it is occurring, the more likely we are to create conditions that will solve it. Simply put, we express the traditional American confidence that insight into the nature of a particular problem will give practical directions to specific solutions.

Continuous improvement in schools is based on improving the learning of individuals. This requires a democratic process of collaborative inquiry informed by the value that all children can learn well. Teachers, parents, and principals in each of our schools enter into spirited dialogue about the progress of their students, collect data about their strengths and weaknesses in learning, agree on specific priorities for improvement, devise and try out solutions, and monitor results. In this way, we are making significant progress engaging schools in the pragmatic process of creating conditions that help students correct the difficulties they are encountering in their efforts to learn. Local school problem solving promotes careful thought about all students and builds a community of professionals who help each other help children learn more.

Local Decision Making

The Constitution of the United States assigns responsibility for public education to the states, which create local boards of education responsible for the instruction of the children of each city, town, and village across the country. Despite a 20th-century fascination with top-down, centralized decision making, our country relegates the federal government to the sidelines of education. For example, we have no national curriculum, no agreed-on assessment program for each level of schooling, and no common certification system for teachers and administrators. This radical stance against centralized control expresses a historical aversion to domination by outside powers.

Yet, there persists a failure to translate this fourth democratic value of local decision making all the way through to the individual school. Although there is more talk in the 1990s of school-based management, the necessity for each school to set its own course is often violated. Teachers and principals with whom we work fight hard to restore greater autonomy for decision making in local schools and the immediate communities they serve. Joining with parents and interested leaders in the neighborhood, educators seek the responsibility and authority to define priorities for the learning of their students. Recognizing that each school has a special culture, they work to assess their own resources and practices while developing and testing solutions to learning problems.

Another challenge is to build a local capacity to evaluate progress, so that continuous improvement directed by the professionals in the school and others is solidly in place. In the democratic tradition of local decision making, the momentum established in the school to increase learning should be supported by administrators in the central office and members of the local community and not dictated by them. This is important to acknowledge because too many education bureaucrats, state politicians, and business leaders use the buzzword "accountability" as a rationale for imposing their policies and priorities, without regard for the creative intelligence of professional educators. This democratic value of local decision making means that those closest to children (classroom teachers, school principals, concerned parents and guardians) are key leaders for improving schools and increasing learning.

Closing

It is time to return to first principles in public education, to consider the ideals of democracy as a starting point for crucial decisions about the renewal of public schools in the United States. Unless we build from tested values emphasizing education as a moral imperative, respect for individuals, pragmatic problem solving, and local control, we run the risk of developing schools that are profoundly inadequate to the challenges of these times. If we overemphasize technical and economic rationales for school reform, our analysis of education's shortcomings will miss the power and urgency that come from working toward the ideal of equality. If we concentrate too much on the accomplishments of the academic elite as our criterion for success, we narrow our vision for excellence and limit our expectations to a narrow range of talents that fall far short of the potential our diverse people possess. If we vainly seek national models for uniform changes in local schools and persistently impose packaged instructional programs to solve the learning problems particular to youngsters in each school, we miss out on the opportunity to tap the creative intelligence of the parents and educators who are closest to the children having difficulty with their learning. Finally, if we succumb to the temptation to impose outside standards, curricula, and testing programs on individual schools and communities, we violate cherished traditions of local control—and to little avail.

The important challenge facing educators and citizens is to help America's public schools live up to their bright promise as the gateways to equality and opportunity. By looking to the strengths of our diverse culture, we seek approaches to school improvement consistent with democratic values. It is in our public schools that children reach their academic and personal promise, and it is through our public schools that each generation learns to take responsibility for continuing the quest of the United States for effective democracy with high-quality education at the center of equality.

References

Adler, M. J. (1982). *The Paideia proposal: An educational manifesto.* New York: Macmillan.

Barber, B. R. (1995). Workshops of our democracy. *Education Week, 14,* 34.

Dewey, J. (1916). *Democracy and education.* New York: The Free Press.

Maier, D. (1995, April 19). Democracy is not always convenient. *Education Week,* 35.

Park, D. N., & Boyd, W. L. (1994). Anti politics, education, and institutional choice: The flight from democracy. *American Educational Research Journal, 31,* 263-281.

Walker, R. (1996, November 15). *Oppression and the human spirit* [author's lecture notes]. Invited address presented at the conference Educating Tibetan Youth: Creating Leaders and Realizing Independence sponsored by the National Coalition for Equality in Learning, Hampshire College, Amherst, MA.

2 *Moral Imperatives of Leadership*

ROBBIE JEAN WALKER

The privilege and responsibility of helping others learn well have engaged the energies and passions of generations. This universal human endeavor has spawned numerous, often conflicting, views of what constitutes an appropriate education. Theories of leading, learning, and teaching proliferate. But the nature of the task retains familiar parameters. Public education is the means by which nations help individuals build meaningful and coherent lives amid competing agendas and diverse social circumstances. This astounding expectation has challenged educational leadership across time. Such a monumental mission must be informed by unyielding beliefs against which we evaluate our challenging work to help all children learn well. These beliefs are not rules of practice but principles of conscience.

As leaders of the National Coalition for Equality in Learning, we understand the necessity of guiding principles. It is because appropriate decisions for increasing learning are so closely connected with context that we do not promote specific strategies. Rather, our leadership is based on several moral imperatives. It is to these imperatives that the content of this chapter is directed.

Recently rereading portions of Adolphe E. Meyer's *Grandmasters of Educational Thought* (1975), I was astounded to see how well the motivations and passions of our work to ensure equality in education comported with traditions espoused by the grandmasters. Although we do—and should—put a modern face on many principles conceived in a cultural past, we embrace many of the notions of the grandmasters such as Plato, who believed that children's lives would be ennobled by exposing them to the presence of beauty (p. 29); Jean-Jacques Rousseau, who argued that teachers need to "know" the children they teach (p. 48); Erasmus, who saw the main task of education to go beyond the production of people who know to people who can think and feel (p. 79); John Locke, who advocated "a sound mind in a sound body" (p. 29); and Quintilian, who emphasized "the importance of the home, the child's early education," the peculiar nature of the individual child, and "the value of play and joy as spurs to learning . . . not from books alone, but from experience as well" (pp. 51-52).

From these bedrocks of educational thought, collective experiences, and the challenges that each day brings, responsible educational leaders at all levels recognize the necessity of challenging conventional assumptions, ferreting out promising educational innovations, and evaluating systematically what is true and relevant and responsible in educating the youth of this country. Leadership is ever evolving for numerous reasons. We learn from our mistakes, and the creativity of children never ceases to impose an inevitable—and necessary—sense of humility. Our construction of ultimate possibilities continues to elude us as we see some of our greatest efforts falling short of our dreams. Thus, our practice is always evolving, always in process—as are our learning and professional growth. This disposition to adjust to realities as we find them, however, is not attributable to lack of focus or confused sense of purpose. Rather, our practices are invariably based on unnegotiable beliefs about the human spirit, the development of children, and the attainment of excellence.

The concept of leadership, in its potential and ideal state, encompasses considerations that are both comprehensive and inclusive. Superintendents, principals, boards of education, and other administrators generally assume a centralized leadership that lends focus and coherence to the system they serve. Yet, there is a unique and commendable characteristic of leaders in the National Coalition that is more inclusive than traditional leadership as they seek to help children of all families succeed in school. Although traditional positions of leadership receive well-deserved respect, the challenges and prestige of leadership are also accorded to classroom teachers, who are pivotal in decision making and implementation of innovations. An organization of educators committed to equality considers any-one engaged in the monumental task of helping children learn as a legitimate leader. Therefore, it is to the convergence of all these layers of leadership that we refer when we speak of moral imperatives, as the ultimate worth of all that we seek to do in schools and classrooms across the country translates in one way or another to that magic occurring in interactions between teachers and learners.

Meeting Needs of All Learners

One prominent moral postulate guiding effective leadership is a belief in the fundamental right of every child to be respected and challenged to the extent of his or her ability. In a country as diverse as ours, with a national psyche committed to individual rights and development, myriad political causes and social agendas command our consideration. The unfortunate irony in education is that the very effectiveness of our mission sometimes becomes fragmented by our compassion for specific agendas. Perhaps some temporary fragmen-tation is inevitable as we concentrate our energies on specific or immediate crises—as well we should. But we recognize our chal-lenge to put all of the pieces back together again when we begin to contemplate the concrete realities to be invoked while we try to educate all the youth of this democratic country.

Pivotal considerations here are sound judgment and balance. When we hear the genuine appeal for children living in adverse circumstances, for example, we have the professional and moral obligation to respond with all the resources at our command. And when we hear the plea for cultural tolerance, we need to call forth all the principles of decency and inclusion to avert indelible negative experiences that alienate and diminish the human spirit. For these reasons, the reality of individual differences lies at the very core of our educational philosophy. We understand that some will walk with faltering steps, some will sprint, and some will soar. Sound moral leadership in education demands that we recognize and respect these differences, setting appropriate standards for all concerned.

Sometimes, unfortunately, we focus solely on a particular need and exclude all other concerns. The kinds of things we do to educate all children will vary, so our obligation to give every one of them our very best every day has become a password of effective leaders. We acknowledge the fact that our children deserve better than fragmentation deriving from competing agendas that pit one class or race or ability level against another. After all, it will be that textural diversity—representing, as it does, a microcosm of society itself—that will ultimately blend into the complex and beautiful tapestry that characterizes the United States.

Why do we need to educate all? Because each individual contributes a unique essence not found in any other. Why do we need to employ our best efforts at every node on the continuum of the human condition? Because we need the talents and uniqueness of all. Our promise is to tap the reservoir of potential at every level and channel appropriately the rich resources represented in the different groups.

This is why learning communities with which we work view sorting by ability levels with a healthy skepticism and attend to this reality with vigilance, constantly monitoring all dimensions of the learning process and seeking validation—or refutation, if such is indeed indicated—for the assumptions governing their practices. We also witness clear demonstrations of a commendable wisdom that has not always been appropriately honored in all educational communities. Teachers as leaders show appreciation for the differences existing even among children of similar ability levels. They recognize that children may be equally bright or gifted, but that does not mean that they are the same. And they also plan with the reality that high intellectual ability does not suggest that such children be left alone. Rather, teachers embrace the notion that challenge is crucial and that we must respect uniqueness at every level of interaction with all children, ever mindful of nuances that require consideration and adjustment so that learning prevails.

Adjustments are obviously necessary in the case of marginal learners, those youngsters who are disconnected from productive learning. Leaders are committed to furthering the possibilities of the marginal student because they recognize the need for extended efforts as they continuously seek to grant all students access to the promises of the United States. We embrace the responsibility of bridging the gaps and extending the horizons of students who are "at risk" of being permanently on the margins of school success. This effort, though, does not indicate a lack of concern for the gifted or otherwise exceptional. Our goals are not limited to one kind of student. The relevant guiding philosophy is a recognition that students differ in numerous ways and that we must be ever mindful of those who without concentrated effort may well fall short of their potential. Yet, we still feel equally obligated to channel the energies of superior students and challenge them to excel.

It is not ours to create hierarchies and special places—we are not wise enough to predict just when a particular kind of person may save the day. The restless, creative child who challenges our sanity may one day use that restlessness and that creativity to make a contribution of universal significance. That C student may be the one with the perseverance, the care, and the fortitude to make significant contributions that will make the world take notice. That marginal child may one day challenge the status quo in ways we cannot foresee. That is one reason to embrace the professional obligation to address the educational needs of all children of all colors and every family background.

Educating Hearts and Minds

In addition to the moral imperative of leading every child to the limits of his or her intellectual potential, as generally perceived by all responsible educators, National Coalition leaders consider educating both hearts and minds to be a pivotal obligation. Invoking the revered words of Chief Justice of the U.S. Supreme Court Earl Warren and the dramatization of that concept in Harry S. Ashmore's compelling work *Hearts and Minds* (1982), we believe that educational leaders must be the custodians of the spirits as well as the minds of the children with whom they work. The words of the chief justice resound today as clearly as they did when he penned the memorable words in May 1954: "To separate them [children of color] from others of similar age and qualifications solely because of their race generates a feeling of inferiority as to their status in the community that may affect their hearts and minds in ways unlikely to ever be undone" (*Brown v. Board of Education*, 1954, p. 691).

This responsibility to educate both hearts and minds has numerous implications, a prominent one being the realization that intellectual landmarks cannot be erected on the debris of broken spirits. One of several commendable tendencies of classroom teachers as leaders is the care with which they handle the feelings of students. For example, as a member of the national faculty of the National Coalition, I have sat in classrooms across the nation exulting in the respect teachers accorded particular students grappling with a stubborn question. I have observed perhaps a dozen hands raised in eagerness to solve a problem while the teacher waited patiently for one struggling student to experience a moment of triumph. These teachers judiciously recognized one particular child's need for success at a given moment. Reaching for the opportunity for success rather than yielding to the realities of time became the prevailing challenge. Many teachers in similar situations would yield to the realities of time, as indeed all of us must sometimes unfortunately do. But the moments here dramatize the prevailing attitude of outstanding teachers. As leaders empowered with latitude in their dealings with students, they will often risk, if they must, the criticism of what many would refer to as "lost time." To people of lesser confidence, these moments of silence could well loom ominous and become threatening. Yet, teachers confident of the support of their own leaders will risk that seemingly interminable moment of silence to encourage a child who needs this one success now.

This attention to "hearts and minds" is rendered concrete in the attitudes of those leaders who have made the word *limitations* a part of another language, another time. Thus, we accept our obligation to lead all students to a form of learning that is characterized by depth and texture. A common denominator of educational excellence and positive self-esteem is that of high expectations. We communicate to students in many ways exactly what we think of them as people: whether or not we think they are able learners, whether or not we believe in their ultimate worth, whether or not we respect their personhood, whether or not we consider them equal and deserving heirs of the promises that our democracy claims to embrace. We touch more than their minds when we set forth high expectations. We communicate implicitly how much we value our students' ability and promise.

Some trends in education and curricula, embraced by people who claim to know, have greatly affected how children are taught. At given points in our history, educational leaders decided that some children needed easier books, and a different kind of reading was recommended for them. That was a time when followers failed to stop and take a look at one of the common denominators traditionally characteristic of public education—high expectations. A refreshing attitude of leaders is that they reject many of the traditional notions of gatekeeping. They do not deny students of adverse circumstances exposure to the beauty and grace of language or enriching experiences. Nor do they consider the lilting magic of words as demonstrated in the classics to be the sole right of the academically anointed.

This does not suggest that we have bought into some kind of elitism; nor have we ignored culturally different concerns. What we have done is to embrace as a moral imperative of leadership an attitude based on hopes and possibilities, an attitude that acknowledges the spirit as well as the intellect. Expectations are the ceilings we erect, the tangible and intangible representation of how much we value the students we teach. We believe that all learning needs connections, a coherent unity of the discrete dimensions that make up learning and meaning. Rote exercises and drill can never satisfy our students' deepest yearnings and aspirations. Corrective drill at appropriate points in the learning process is appropriate pedagogy, but rote exercises and drill are limiting when too broadly applied, when they become the emphasis and end of our efforts to help our children learn well.

We affect both the hearts and minds of our students when we make assumptions based on external circumstances. This is often the conventional wisdom in dealing with children of poverty. Effective leaders accept the moral imperative to challenge children of all circumstances. We understand that there are realities about being poor. There are fewer books in the home library, if any at all. There is less money to travel to places that other students can talk about firsthand. These realities mean that a given student will not know the meaning of many words with which children from a different, more benevolent, set of circumstances are readily conversant. The challenge of leaders is that of avoiding the assumption that children of poverty cannot learn. At the same time, educators are cognizant of the need to provide background information subtly and respectfully so that children of poverty and limited experiences may also enjoy the texture and depth of varied learning experiences. Poverty is real, but too many damaging myths are attached to poverty. And over time, these myths have made a difference in the ways we try to help children learn. The myths of poverty do not deal with whether or not poverty exists, for all of us know that it does. Rather, the crucial question is: What, precisely, does poverty mean in a learning community?

Productive learning communities constantly and consciously evaluate their attitudes about children of poverty. What kind of leadership will it take for the children of poverty to realize their potential? Poverty is often accorded more power than it deserves. We are finding that poverty is a condition that defies strict parameters and certainties. Too often, people forget that poverty is just that—a condition. It has no irreversible link to morality or lack of it. It has no direct link to intelligence, though it logically may have a direct link to achievement if we allow it to. What we seek is leadership that avoids making inappropriate generalizations and assumptions about children who are poor. Teachers as leaders know that when we allow poverty to deter learning, we further entrench the conditions we are obligated to counteract.

We challenge leaders to reexamine the very makeup of the word *socioeconomic*. To us, this term carries some very damaging assumptions. It suggests that how much money people have or the circumstances in which they live have an inevitable impact on their dreams and aspirations. The *economic* part of the term addresses the financial circumstances. But *socio* is a much more insidious formulation that people use far too carelessly. For tied up in that designation is a vast array of assumptions. It includes the value systems and the daily lives of children. Thus, when we consider excluding limitations from our language of hope, we do so with an understanding of and appreciation for the reality of circumstances. The difference between our views and some other current notions is what we think and do about varied circumstances. We do not pretend that those we teach will not differ. What we categorically reject, though, is the notion that we have either the wisdom or authority to apply untested assumptions to children of any circumstance. Diverse circumstances do not dictate unequal destinies. But honoring the imperative of educating hearts as well as minds ensures that we avoid the destruction of children's spirits and the concomitant negation of the possibility of their realizing their promise.

Making Learning a Lifelong Commitment

Another imperative of leadership is the humbling acknowledgment that our learning is not—and can never be—complete. Effective leaders are continuing learners. Tentativeness and the willingness to continue to evaluate the status and sufficiency of our knowledge and the progress of the young people we serve is not tantamount to acknowledging incompetence. Technically, every age in our history has been an age of information explosion, maybe not so astounding as the current explosion—but exploding nonetheless. Professional development is a way of life for those who assume the monumental task of helping children learn. Knowledge has its own built-in continuity, its own relationship to what has gone before. Our students will know things that we do not know. Again, this reality should not be a source of shame, for the substantive concern is our ability to help students continue what Robert Hutchins (1952) termed the "great conversation." This means that we will lead them to a level of competence at which they can commune with the great minds of the past and also make their own contributions to abundant learning and constructive living.

Educators who do not continue to learn are the ones without confidence, the ones who flinch when a student proffers a bit of information with which they are not familiar. These colleagues feel that the failure to know a particular fact is an indication of insufficiency. Those leaders who continue to learn more fully appreciate the vast repositories of knowledge and accept, albeit reluctantly, that they will never possess all knowledge. What effective leaders commit themselves to, however, is a consistent hunger for ideas and an enduring spirit of inquiry. Viewed in this way, we do not become intimidated by discrete facts that we do not know. Rather, we gain confidence if we maintain a commitment to continuing learning, secure in the fact that because we are still learning, we can never be summarily limited or completely defined. The notion of leaders as learners, then, is a conceptual possibility that attributes another dimension to our professionalism.

A recent article in *Teacher Magazine* dramatizes the need for and potential of continuing learning and renewal. One teacher commented: "The highest priority for policy makers and administrators who want to improve public education should be to liberate teachers from these restraints [those innumerable tasks that consume so much of teachers' time] and unleash their enormous potential to bring our schools into the next century" (Wolk, 1996, p. 3). Unleashing that potential is of utmost importance, an imperative in responding to professional needs and providing renewal for teachers. Teachers daily confront an amalgam of astounding expectations. No other professional is expected to respond to the needs of all of the participants in a group setting at the same time. This tremendous and unusual commitment requires time for preparation and renewal. Such concerns are not foreign to successful learning communities in the National Coalition. We visited several communities and marveled at the creativity demonstrated by administrators in providing opportunities for teachers to attend to reflection and learning. Some school boards, for example, hired substitutes for a day or more to give teachers the opportunity to withdraw from the inevitable stresses of their daily obligations and to reflect on the specifics of their responsibilities or review their philosophical assumptions.

Progressive learning communities do not perceive professional development opportunities as a waste of the taxpayers' money. Rather, time for learning and renewal is a humane and effective demonstration of care, a formal acknowledgment that the noble mission of teaching can indeed be enhanced by reflection. The net result is a group of teachers returning to their work with higher morale and a greater determination to do their very best for the children they teach and their colleagues who care. Implicit in the obligation to continue learning is the imperative that leaders provide an opportunity to continue learning.

Establishing and Maintaining an Atmosphere of Trust

Signs designating "safe places" will no doubt be applauded for years to come as an eloquent testimonial to the humane spirit of this generation. The concept acknowledges the psychological need for safety, a precondition for accomplishment in a multitude of circumstances. Thus, another moral imperative informing efforts of the leadership we advocate is that all children should feel safe, protected, and affirmed. Educational leaders are morally obligated to establish and maintain a climate of trust in all learning communities. Children need to feel confident that they can engage in the joys and wonders of learning without ridicule or censure. Sometimes, evolving thought is so fragile and the risk to share it is so formidable that students often leave classes and grade levels without the confidence to test their ideas.

Effective leaders demonstrate a tolerance for second chances, the patience to encourage a child in the process of attempting to impose order on a chaotic thought. This willingness to wait will teach children a much-needed patience indispensable to anyone who deals seriously with ideas and inquiry. Some concrete guidelines obtain in establishing a community of trust. For example, trust will come if a student never sees another student ridiculed or humiliated for not getting something completely right the first time, never witnesses a student response scoffed at or ridiculed by a teacher, or never sees an honest effort go unrewarded. As with all other aspects of learning, all students will not suddenly arrive one day at a level of complete trust, nor will any one student show complete consistency in risk taking. But an atmosphere of trust becomes a breeding place for the fledgling thought that will one day take full flight.

We should never underestimate the importance of physical safety to children. The challenge for leadership, though, is to make safety all-encompassing—to include the spirits of children as we help them to learn. As much as we seek to avoid failure, it will inevitably occur in a learning environment. What children need is the belief that they can fail with dignity; they need to know that their mistakes will not be magnified. They need to feel safe from physical harm, and they need to feel safe from emotional damage.

An environment of trust can make the difference between a student trying again or giving up in defeat. Such an atmosphere emboldens students to experiment with ideas, to grapple with concepts about which they are not certain. Leaders and educators committed to developing a lifelong love for learning and a belief in the rewards of effort must ensure that children are free to learn, free to fail, and free to try again. Children will not thrive educationally when they fear ridicule or rejection, when our actions communicate to them something less than our belief in their ability to succeed.

A positive self-concept pays high dividends. Children who value themselves and feel that they are valued will be more considerate of everyone around them. They will have no need to lash out or to "prove" their worth. And they will learn these things from the climate we create in our learning communities. The safety spawned from the affirmation of a committed teacher and considerate peers will last more than one day or one year. All our accumulation of knowledge, our mastery of strategies, and our neatly penned plans will be negated if we fail to make school a place our students love and one to which they are eager to return.

How do we seek to instill hope so that it becomes more powerful than the contrary forces permeating students' lives? We set high goals, we hold forth great expectations, we challenge, and we nurture. We learn not to link oppressive conditions with possibilities. This is no easy task, for we must invoke two challenging actions, each one demanding in its own right. We must provide a cocoon of safety so that despair will not engulf our children. Yet, we must also create enough dissatisfaction to make them want to realize the ultimate. The road may be long and meandering, but they need to be assured that it leads finally to refreshing streams and peaceful meadows. We need not pretend that every day will be a picnic beside refreshing streams or a walk through peaceful meadows. But they need to know that there are such things.

Acknowledging and Understanding the Resiliency of the Human Spirit

As leaders and educators, we embrace our responsibility to compensate for negative societal influences vying for the morale and dignity of our students. Such vigilance is commendable, but it does not take into account intangibles that enable some students to succeed in spite of adversity, in spite of troubled homes, in spite of oppression. Some cultures and individuals demonstrate a remarkable capacity to confront obstacles—a determination to defy predictions. Although we do not completely understand this phenomenon, we should nurture this resiliency to the extent of our ability. This is another moral imperative of leadership.

We need to do more than encourage these intangibles. Interacting with students and giving them opportunities for open-ended responses can assist us in identifying the attributes that feed the hearts and minds of our students, even in circumstances of great difficulty. Respect for and acknowledgment of these factors of resiliency deserve careful observation and analysis. It may well be that understanding the intricacies of this phenomenon can be of great significance and relevance in our work with all students.

Responding to Moral Imperatives of Leadership

The educators we work with across the country are joined together in an organization of hope and action. This organization is intended to make real the promise of those courageous Americans who first believed in the possibility that this country could educate all its citizens. Participants in this organization have not lost hope in the nation's youth and believe that with the best leadership we can give, we will be rewarded with an informed and civil populace capable of conducting the affairs of this country. We believe in educating hearts and minds, to recall Ashmore's words, rendered compellingly concrete in Margaret Walker Alexander's speech before the National Urban League in 1968. In that address, Alexander argued, "For the great possession of money without guiding principles, without judgment, without pride and integrity, such possession is nothing . . . . that cars and houses and whiskey and clothes and all the trappings of an affluent society do not dress up empty minds, and ugly hearts, and loveless lives" (Alexander, 1968/1992, p. 323). Our dream, then, is one of an educated populace, competitive with any nation in the world, yet a populace that complements its academic mission with appropriate attention to the moral and emotional needs of all its citizens.

We believe that we can make a difference in the lives of all children. We entertain no illusions about equal ability, but we tenaciously defend equality of opportunity and commit ourselves to meeting the needs of a diverse citizenry. We believe that teaching is always an invocation of magic, that the meeting of minds that takes place when we connect with those we teach is a phenomenon we are unable to describe. Yet, we believe in the mystery of learning and the wonder of making the world a better place. We believe that what we do in the nation's classrooms every day will affect eternity—for good or ill. In view of the magnitude of this reality, we remain an organization of action, for we believe that the mere recitation of principles is insufficient for the nobility of our mission. We are guided by principles of fairness and morality, and we know that we must be active agents in working toward making these ideals a reality.

We make no attempt to codify strategies, nor are we so presumptuous as to recommend definitive educational practices for all schools. We do believe, however, that the application of sound principles and good judgment will inevitably influence what we do in the name of education. Cognizant of the diverse situations encountered by educators, we believe that posterity will record what effect we have had on the environments in which we have dwelt and worked. Jay L. Robinson's assertion in a recent issue of *On Common Ground* comports well with our philosophy: "No structural organization is ever likely to be as important as are the changes we can make in the ways we perceive and respond to one another as human beings" (1996, p. 15).

If we could, as did Langston Hughes in his masterful poem, dream a world, it would be one in which all children felt as safe and as affirmed in school every day as we do in our work. Our objectives are not complex, but the work is ever evolving because the needs of the children we teach are diverse and unpredictable. We respect the unique nature of each child and every learning situation. Thus, the most apt characterization of our philosophical stance is "evolving." Although the National Coalition exercises a level of flexibility and tentativeness in its work, it attains a coherence deriving from basic moral imperatives, some of which have been discussed in this chapter.

The tentativeness we feel is not an indication of insecurity or lack of focus. Rather, we accept the high probability that we will learn more and more. And as we learn, integrity dictates that we either adapt or reaffirm. Thus our engagement is always active. Reevaluation for us does not always mean change. In many instances, we find the wisdom of our educational efforts confirmed. Yet, in other cases, we may find that we are searching for solutions where there are no problems. The wellspring of our constant evaluation is our commitment to seek the truth about learning. We have no illusions that this search will end with us. Continuing that search with a view toward giving all our children the best we are capable of giving is the living dream of leaders who seek the reality of equality.

References

Alexander, M. W. (1992). Religion, poetry, and history. In R. J. Walker (Ed.), *The rhetoric of struggle: Public address by African American Women* (pp. 311-324). New York: Garland. (Original address given in 1968)

Ashmore, H. S. (1982). *Hearts and minds: The anatomy of racism from Roosevelt to Reagan.* New York: McGraw-Hill.

Brown v. Board of Education, 347 U.S. 483, 74 S.Ct. 686 (1954).

Hutchins, R. M. (1952). *The great conversation: The substance of a liberal education.* Chicago: Encyclopædia Britannica.

Meyer, A. E. (1975). *Grandmasters of educational thought.* New York: McGraw-Hill.

Robinson, J. L. (1996, Spring). University-school collaboration and educational reform. *On Common Ground, 6,* 15.

Wolk, R. (1996, August). Connections: Untapped potential. *Teacher Magazine, 7*(9), 3.

Learning Lessons of Change 3

KIMBERLY TRIMBLE

JAN JACOB

It is the very end of the day. I look up as Cheryl enters the room. "How was the workshop?" I asked. Cheryl rolls her eyes as she slumps into a chair. "You know the definition of an experienced teacher?" she asks, repeating the setup line of a standard teachers'-room joke. I chuckled, for as an 18-year veteran, I had heard the quip many times before. "Someone who's been hit by the same pendulum twice. Right?" I volunteered. She shook her head, sighing softly before speaking, "What a waste of 2 hours! I would have done a lot better if I had spent the time grading papers."

A wonderfully talented teacher, several times recognized by the school and the district as an outstanding educator, Cheryl is returning from the district's mandatory inservice meeting where a local university professor gave a presentation on improving students' test scores to the middle school staff. At the meeting, the staff were informed that the school had adopted a packaged program meant to prepare students for the eighth-grade statewide test given each spring. Cheryl's experience is hardly unique. Throughout the country, teachers like her are bracing themselves as cadres of policymakers, university professors, and educational consultants gear up for another round of frenzied school reform.

Rarely in the history of our country have the pressures for public schools to change been so widespread or the critics so vocal. This attention from politicians and the public at large should not be surprising, given the social and economic uncertainties that seem to mark the last several years. The growing homelessness among school-age students, the dramatic levels of teenage pregnancies, and the drug use devastating more and more families have forced governments at all levels to redesign social and economic programs that might address these problems. In the search for someone or something that will respond to these unsettling conditions, the public seems to be looking to schools—one of the few institutions that still has widespread popular support (McDermott & Trimble, 1993)—to address this incredible range of social problems.

Though schools cannot deal directly with the social and economic realities that create homelessness, poverty, displacement, and despair, all of these conditions affect children's learning. Students coming from these adverse circumstances often arrive at the school door ill fed, sick, suffering from abuse or neglect, and exhibiting short attention spans, low motivation, and severe learning difficulties. Classroom chairs are also increasingly filled by students from homes where English is not commonly spoken. For many of these students, the added insecurity of undocumented or illegal residency status poses additional burdens to school success. This is the reality too many teachers face daily.

But as Cheryl's reaction suggests, recycling previous reform efforts is unlikely to change dramatically what teachers do in schools— or what children learn. Fundamental changes in school, changes that alter the way in which teachers, students, parents, and administrators interact, go beyond merely intensifying what already exists in classrooms. Nor is restructuring the school's organization a powerful means for helping children from adverse circumstances learn well. We find that reorganizing schools does not change how people think or act toward each other. *Restructuring* is a word that will soon be considered unfashionable, and it should be replaced with thoughtful actions that center on increasing learning in local schools. Creating conditions so that all children learn well, no matter what troubling issues they face, is the venture educators must undertake.

In this chapter, we will discuss the work of schools that are addressing these key issues in ways that question many basic assumptions about schools and the people who live and learn in them. Working from the premise that all students should experience successful learning, teachers and administrators develop a shared process for school improvement to make classrooms accessible and meaningful to all students. From the experiences of diverse schools arise critical understandings about this process of change. When carefully examined, these lessons contradict many traditional tenets of how individuals in schools and the broader community may help children improve their learning. Based on the dedicated efforts to make schools places where all students can succeed, they cast a focused and illuminating light on the present discussion of necessary directions for public education.

Structural Resistance to Change

With their buildings, telephone networks, payrolls, and governing boards, modern schools seem to resemble other large organizations in our society, such as businesses or corporations. Despite such outward trappings, however, schools are remarkably similar in most fundamental ways to their turn-of-the-century predecessors. Jackson (1968), Cuban (1984), Goodlad (1984), and a host of other educational observers have documented the enduring nature of life in schools over the past 100 years despite the periodic throngs of enthusiastic critics bent on transforming schools.

To understand this resistance to change, it is useful to note how schools differ from other large, contemporary institutions. From their inception, schools were given an unusual mandate: to pass on to young people a sense of communal responsibility and the skills to contribute productively to the society. In responding to this task, schools bring together an uncommonly broad range of people from differing ages, social classes, and cultural backgrounds in ways quite rare in most organizations. Furthermore, as the society became increasingly complex, schools were asked to assume an ever-expanding responsibility for an array of diverse social tasks. As a result, schools often struggled to maintain clearly articulated purposes like those that motivate people to interact in businesses or social groupings (Trimble, 1996).

Although change, especially in complex social institutions, can be exceedingly slow and painful, the organizational structures of schools seem to be especially effective in reinforcing the status quo and confounding attempts to change. Separated into individual classrooms, following rigid time schedules, and surrounded by young people, teachers are routinely secluded from others who also practice the profession. Such independence is valued by many teachers, but this isolation does little to create a common vision among educators that would encourage careful examination of problems or changes of conditions in schools. This privacy of practice is often even more exaggerated in secondary schools, where large teaching staffs are divided into academic departments.

The public nature of school governance also discourages creativity and innovation. With their policies and decisions open to public debate at monthly board meetings, school administrators operate far more publicly than their business counterparts and are more susceptible to prevailing political and educational winds. Though parental and community monitoring fosters accountability, this scrutiny tends to make administrators wary of changes that might be unconventional or controversial. This resistance to change frustrates many reformers, but the success of our efforts is based in large part on educators' abilities to recognize these conditions and realities of schools and use them to reinforce desired change. As teachers and administrators work to help students who are marginalized in their learning by traditional classroom policies and practices, they seek approaches to change that are effective in the existing school environment and develop new roles for educators and parents where institutional routines made meaningful change unlikely.

Locating Educational Expertise: Looking for Change in All the Wrong Places

Over the course of their work together, educators in National Coalition schools found themselves reconsidering several common assumptions about the nature of school improvement. One of the most valuable lessons to emerge, one that contrasts sharply with many other change endeavors, concerns the nature of educational problems and solutions. As Cheryl's story suggests, school reform in this country is marked by its cyclical nature, with periods of intense interest in schools followed by times of relative neglect. What also characterizes educational improvement, however, is that the impetus for change often originates outside of schools. Many recent reform movements have their roots in political or social events in the broader society. The launching of the Soviet satellite *Sputnik,* for example, began a frenzied period of reform in the late 1950s and the 1960s, just as more recent social and economic concerns engendered heated debate on school vouchers, phonetics, and math instruction.

Reformers also tend to look beyond the classroom door for solutions to real or perceived problems in schools. As Roland Barth (1990) points out, knowledge for school improvement has historically been derived from large-scale social science research rather than from educators who reside in the schools. Yet, we are finding that it is productive to seek the experiences of classroom teachers and administrators in determining directions for change.

As might be expected, efforts to introduce external solutions to internal problems show little regard for those who work daily in schools. Traditional approaches to improvement, based on authoritarian conceptions of change, assume that existing practices are responsible for students' failures. According to this thinking, teachers, who through ignorance or obstinacy adhere to outmoded strategies, should be encouraged or, if necessary, coerced into changing their classroom behavior. Indeed, what may most distinguish reform movements since the Second World War—from new math to whole language to back-to-basics—is the impositions of solutions on local educators regardless of the nature of the problems that students might be experiencing.

Our work with educators in local schools differs clearly from other reform efforts that locate the solution to educational problems outside of schools. Colleagues come to understand that solutions must flow from a careful understanding of the learning problem. Those individuals most familiar with the unique attributes and needs of the students must help shape solutions. Teachers, who are in daily contact with students and have personal knowledge of their problems, are perhaps the best positioned to suggest and design productive changes in the learning environment.

A meaningful understanding of students' problems usually emerges when educators engage in a process of collaborative inquiry. Educators who work with us develop and refine a common strategy called the "study team." A powerful tool for gathering information and gaining knowledge about learning problems, the study team brings together teachers, administrators, and occasionally parents and community members to investigate the particular difficulties students are facing. By concentrating on students' experiences in the classroom and school, the study team can peel back the layers of the learning problem to expose root causes, as well as symptoms. Only after study team participants develop a firm grasp of these problems do they turn their attention to ways to address difficulties children experience.

Because complex understandings are gained in study teams, educators become especially wary of packaged curricula or predetermined strategies, which are developed with no knowledge of the particular needs of their own students. Although national trends for reform may be useful in suggesting possible directions for action, they do little to guide educators to improve learning in their local schools. If, after extended dialogue and problem analysis, particular approaches (to reading or mathematics, for example) offer promising solutions to learning problems, they might be tried for a period in the school. Whatever solutions are implemented, they reflect a great deal of professional thought and analysis rather than an imposition or mechanical adoption of the latest canned curriculum.

In addition to creating conditions specifically tailored to student learning problems in each school, this cooperative approach to problem solving has other beneficial aspects. As educators in a study team gain knowledge and expertise through the process of inquiry, confidence in their own abilities to address the needs of their students increases. The isolation and resistance that frequently occurs in imposed change is dramatically reduced, as teachers are involved in defining and developing specific solutions to particular learning problems. Collaborative inquiry also prevents the fragmented approaches to teaching children that so often result when teachers do not share ideas or have opportunities to discuss successes and failures with their peers.

Educational Leadership: Not Enough Chiefs

Another important lesson from our work across the country concerns the nature of leadership needed to improve public schooling. Although reformers often lament the resistance to change, frequently blaming teachers for the failure of reform efforts, our educators note that weak leadership often discourages teachers from working to alter schools. Traditionally, for example, curriculum and instruction decisions are made in central offices and passed down to principals and teachers for implementation. These include broad guidelines for what is to be learned at each grade, as well as general suggestions for instructional materials and sequencing of learning experiences. Such a general structure may be useful to guide teachers' decision making. What has become increasingly common, however, is the imposition of specific instructional strategies and classroom activities on teachers.

Conventional professional development programs clearly illustrate how teachers are marginalized in instructional decision making. In most school districts, a certain number of days are set aside for professional development. Educational consultants (often university professors or former school administrators) or central office staff present curriculum packages or instructional techniques that teachers are then expected to use in their classrooms. Hesitation by teachers to use what is suggested is often viewed as resistance to change.

As Cheryl's story points out, an approach to professional development that is imposed by leadership from the top can easily engender anger and resentment from teachers, who often are unconvinced that they need to be "developed" and are sure that they are not being treated professionally. These imposed practices isolate and diminish the kind of knowledge teachers possess and provide few opportunities for teachers to change schooling directly. Excluded from the decisions about these forced reforms, teachers often feel compelled to protect their students from innovations that they think will hinder their learning. Cast in the role of resisters, many teachers find their energies consumed in deflecting reform efforts that are inappropriate for their classrooms, rather than in developing more effective ways to help students learn. Educators in the schools where we work attempt to avoid these pitfalls. As they discover that traditional hierarchical structures and established roles make meaningful change difficult, there are important shifts in leadership responsibilities. This is especially true for teachers who have played a much more central role in creating learning environments that are conducive to student success.

Study teams, then, serve as important avenues for channeling the powerful leadership potential of teachers. Teachers use the expertise gained from working in their own classrooms to address problems learners experience throughout the school. Participating in this process of questioning and dialogue, teachers gain expertise in analyzing problems and build skill in searching for effective solutions. This collaborative process of dialogue provides opportunities for individuals—both teachers and administrators—to work together in ways quite distinct from established routines in most schools. Many districts, such as Spring, Texas; Boulder, Colorado; and Montgomery, Alabama, realize that study teams can reduce teacher isolation, create opportunities for effective teacher decision-making, and foster constructive teacher leadership.

Beyond simply discussing issues, however, teachers take increased responsibility for implementing their ideas. This is a critical step in school change, as teachers must have occasions to practice leadership if effective solutions to students' problems are to be implemented. Increasingly, teachers assume responsibility for planning and carrying out study teams. This may include identifying outside individuals who could provide specific technical information that would advance the group's inquiry about students' learning, but study team planners more frequently draw on the experiences of other educators in their school or district. The teachers do not think solutions to learning problems are outside themselves. Rather, they believe that it is insight into a specific learning problem that results in productive solutions. We are finding that educators do not improve student learning by imitating other people's successes. Progress made elsewhere may illuminate crucial problems and highlight possible solutions in local settings, but lasting and meaningful improvements come from careful identification of problems children are having in the teacher's own classroom and school. Students cannot learn by proxy and leadership, for learning does not happen by imitation.

Teachers also expand their leadership in professional development. With the restructuring of their classrooms to ensure learning by all students, teachers expose conventionally organized staff development as inadequately addressing their needs. As a result, teachers now work closely with administrators to plan and often present experiences that provide knowledge and foster skills that forward the process of improvement in their classrooms (Trimble, 1996). In local schools, the invaluable resource that teachers represent may be nurtured by providing opportunities for teachers to continue to learn while remaining in the classroom with children. Here, leadership becomes, as Sinclair and Ghory (1987) suggest, a function and not a position.

Innovative school principals play a critical role in these emerging patterns of leadership. The principals act on a powerful idea that people, not policy, improve student learning. Realizing that schools cannot become better at serving students without first developing the people in them, principals encourage entire staffs to work together for school improvement. By creating environments that invite broad participation in setting priorities, changing conditions in schools and classrooms that hinder learning, and maintaining those that foster learning, principals move away from controlling change to supporting ideas and facilitating teacher leadership. This seems to stop the pendulum from hitting twice.

Principals use study teams to help redefine their leadership role in the local schools. Drawing on schoolwide resources, they work to ensure that teachers have the time and freedom to investigate and pursue "home-brewed" approaches to solving students' learning problems. They also provide encouragement to participants, urging them to explore problems thoroughly without moving prematurely to a packaged solution and supporting them in broadening their investigation to examine school policies that may be forcing students to the margins of learning. As study teams become increasingly successful in addressing learning difficulties, they reinforce the notion that teaching professionals, using the resources available to them, are very capable of identifying problems students experience in their learning and creating effective ways to help young people resolve their difficulties.

Constructing Democratic Learning Communities

A final lesson that is emerging from our work with public schools is that the ultimate measure of successful school reform is the creation of learning communities that espouse and practice equality. Although educators remain clearly focused upon the intellectual and social development of students, they are aware that educational innovations must engage and benefit all members of the community if the school is to be effective. When broad democratic participation is encouraged in each classroom and across the school, it is more likely that meaningful change will occur. The quality of a school is judged by how well everyone learns, not by the accomplishments of a few who excel while others struggle.

Though the schools we work with differ dramatically in socio-economic class of parents, per student expenditure, and other demographic characteristics, they share certain solid attitudes and ways of viewing schooling that guide them as they seek to develop democratic learning communities based upon equality and fairness. Foremost among these beliefs is the importance of each individual. Unlike many other settings, in which diversity is seen as an obstacle to be overcome, differences among members are prized. These schools tap into the range of experiences, varied viewpoints, careful insights, and special skills of teachers, parents, administrators, and students to enrich the environment for learning.

As solutions to school and social problems require the creativity of everyone involved, parents play an especially important role in schools. Although parental involvement has been given lip service for several decades, parents' roles in joining with the school to promote learning are limited. Most parents are asked simply to attend biannual parent conferences and concerts and occasionally requested to supply food or other services for special events.

We are finding that as educators work to develop caring learning communities, the role of parents is broadened and deepened to enlist their skills and capture their enthusiasm at home and at the school. In schools we serve in Colorado, California, Texas, and elsewhere, parents work directly with teachers as tutors, mentors, and liaisons to other parents. To engage parents productively, educators must listen carefully to parents' ideas about how schools can help them assist in their children's learning. To respond to this need, various schools have parent centers stocked with instructional resources. Usually staffed by parents, these centers help parents make flash cards, storyboards, and other learning aids, as well as check out books and videos to share with their children. Other schools make technology labs available after school, so parents can work on computers with their children.

Many schools carefully step in to address overwhelming social and economic challenges facing parents and other members of the community. Given the reduction of government support, various schools are housing social services on their campuses, providing day care facilities for the children of students, and extending traditional guidance counseling to help with housing and crisis intervention.

Parents also increasingly engage in shaping curriculum and learning decisions in schools and homes. Their involvement provides invaluable insights about how the home and its intricate workings affect the learning of students. This information is critical for framing solutions to learning difficulties. Many schools also seek parents' help in policy decisions as advisory and governance board members.

In democratizing schools, educators turn a critical eye on what and how children are taught. Although teachers recognize that students need to master traditional knowledge to allow access to jobs and higher education, they also realize that typical teaching often works against the democratic community they are trying to build. Without neglecting basic knowledge and skills, they are exploring teaching that furthers the democratic purposes of their classrooms. These democratic adaptations of instruction often begin at the basic level of deciding what is to be taught. Teachers are rejecting conventional teaching that imposes standardized curriculum without cultural considerations and are practicing innovative instruction that builds on the strength of the young people in their care and connects to their lives. In several elementary schools in Boulder, the teachers are involving students in developing curriculum. Teachers note that this fosters independent learning and helps students become self-directed.

Other teachers push beyond basic skills to include critical thinking and abstract analysis in the curriculum. To live in a democratic society and participate thoughtfully in decisions, students must be able to analyze information carefully and consider ideas critically. This may include looking closely at textbooks to identify topics or issues that are excluded or to explore biases presented in their readings and discussions. Teachers also develop opportunities for students to examine bias, propaganda, and slant to engender a critical view of information and how it is used and manipulated.

Educators we work with are concerned about the effects of narrow, tradition-bound curriculum on minority students. Teachers are acutely aware of how the conventional curriculum taught in schools too often minimizes the experiences of many students. In planning curriculum for students, they develop learning experiences that emphasize a variety of voices from points of view that are usually excluded. They often supplement information from textbooks by drawing on the broader community in which students live (parents, local community members, and important historical events) as topics for study.

In many classrooms, students are tapping into the vast reservoir of knowledge located in their community. Observing that young people are often fascinated by events and phenomena they see and hear about daily, teachers create opportunities for students to investigate and make sense of issues and problems that concern them. A study of a polluted local stream in Colorado, for example, allowed students to use science, math, social studies, and language art skills to understand the responsibilities of local industries to protect the environment.

Many teachers are also concerned about the competition that permeates schools and works against collegiality and community among students and teachers. Throughout our participating schools, significant numbers of educators turn to encouraging students to share responsibility and learn from others who are different from themselves. To further cooperation and enable students to work together, many schools are also teaching conflict resolution to their students. In several San Francisco schools, all students are taught negotiation and resolution skills to deal with problems that might arise both in and out of school. Educators also scrutinize existing practices that permeate the entire school as they work to build democratic learning communities. Several practices were identified as barriers to their democratic mission.

In searching to understand students' learning difficulties, many educators realize the limited information that standardized tests offer. These tests generally measure a narrow range of classroom learning, ignoring important instruction and learning that may be more difficult to assess. Furthermore, despite intensive efforts to reduce cultural and racial bias in the exams, many tests still are inappropriate tools for assessing learning of all children. Because of these concerns, many teachers in our schools are using a broader range of information to help them understand students' learning. They find, for example, that actual samples of students' work and direct observation of applied learning are especially useful both in exploring difficulties students may be having and in realizing their strengths.

Educators note that standardized tests are often used to support policies that undermine the creation of communities for learning. In Plymouth Meeting, Pennsylvania, and Victoria, Texas, for example, educators are examining how students are affected by the manner in which they are grouped for instruction. Other schools and districts formed study teams to explore the complex academic and social consequences of grouping students by perceived ability. Many are now pursuing alternatives to ability grouping as they see rigid grouping works against all students reaching high levels of accomplishment (Trimble, 1996). Different criteria for grouping students are being researched. For example, specific skill deficiencies, personal interests, confidence with unknowns, academic strengths, persistence to succeed, and extent of reliance on external reinforcements are criteria that may be used to group students for effective learning.

Closing

Educators in public elementary and secondary schools face continuing challenges to respond to the academic and social needs of the astoundingly diverse groups of students that fill classrooms. Confronted with deep divisions and inequities in society, schools must create citizens carefully schooled in democracy, capable of identifying injustices, and armed with the knowledge and skills to work to change them.

Although the schools we assist across the United States differ dramatically from one another, from a two-room mountain school in Colorado to a modern high school in suburban Minnesota to a middle school in the Hispanic barrio of San Francisco, teachers and administrators all rally to make classrooms meaningful and accessible to all students, especially those children who are pushed to the fringes of productive learning. It is clear that obstacles to student learning are unique to each school setting, and each school has to fashion its distinctive responses after careful study of the learning problems in the context of each local school. In addressing intractable educational problems that frustrate many school improvement efforts, educators must act on their resolute faith in the abilities of colleagues in their local schools to identify and address the difficulties their students experience. This means, as Sinclair and Ghory (1987) urge, going beyond thinking that learning problems are only inside the individual student to examining their own classroom practices, daily procedures, and school policies that may contribute to the students' learning difficulties.

To build lasting and desired changes in public schools, leadership from a broad spectrum of the educational community must emerge, especially from teachers and parents. Through uncharted terrain, dedicated educators in concert with others must move with care and creativity. Their persistent commitment to creating learning communities that espouse and practice equality and to helping all children become productive members of our democracy suggest directions for leading our nation's schools. Our efforts to improve diverse local schools in varied places across the country teach lessons of change that must be learned well if educators and the young people they serve are to meet the challenges of these times.

References

Barth, R. (1990). *Improving schools from within.* San Francisco: Jossey-Bass.

Cuban, L. (1984). *How teachers taught.* New York: Longman.

Goodlad, J. I. (1984). *A place called school.* New York: McGraw-Hill.

Jackson, P. W. (1968). *Life in classrooms.* New York: Holt, Rinehart & Winston.

McDermott, J. C., & Trimble, K. D. (1993, Fall). Neighborhoods as learning laboratories. *California Catalyst,* pp. 28-34.

Sinclair, R. L., & Ghory, W. J. (1987). *Reaching marginal students: A primary concern for school renewal.* Berkeley, CA: McCutchan.

Trimble, K. (1996, April). Building a learning community. *Equity and Excellence in Education, 29*(1), 37-40.

Collaborative Inquiry 4

Teacher Leadership in the Practice of Creative Intelligence

ROBERT G. SMITH

STEPHANIE KNIGHT

Teachers play a key leadership role in making schools and class-rooms places where all young people gain access to a high-quality education. Teachers' knowledge of individual students in particular classrooms places them in the best position to identify problems of student learning and create effective solutions (Sinclair, 1992). Their direct leadership of instruction means they play an important role in altering the environment to increase student learning. Similarly, their engagement with and reflection on the conditions for student learning allow them to generate useful knowledge that improves teaching and advances learning.

Although teachers may certainly engage in problem solving in isolation, our experiences with teachers suggest that collaborative inquiry serves as a particularly powerful vehicle for the exercise of leadership in the improvement of teaching and learning. In working together, teachers practice creative intelligence, as conceived by

39

Dewey (1933), and apply the results of joint reflection on previous experiences with children and instruction to current problems of student learning. External experts and resources may help inform this reflection, but the content and structure of subsequent classroom interventions remain the province of those closest to the problem—classroom teachers working together toward common goals.

As defined in this chapter, collaborative inquiry includes three major components (see Figure 4.1): study teams, teacher research, and peer coaching. Participation in all three encourages teachers to relate research and practice. Inquiry with peers affects teacher thinking and instructional behavior, influences school culture, and improves student learning.

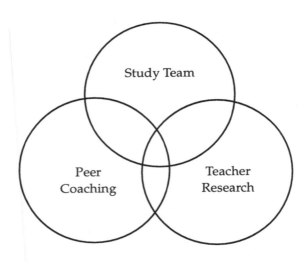

Figure 4.1. The Components of Collaborative Inquiry

Study teams enable teachers to come together for the purposes of identifying and confirming problems of student learning. In teams, teachers also fashion interventions designed to solve problems of student learning. Together, they evaluate the interventions and assess ongoing progress (Smith, 1994).

Study teams are collaborative, but teacher research may be conducted either individually or with colleagues (Patterson, Stansell, &

Lee, 1990). It may serve several purposes related to the study team process. For example, teacher research may help with identifying particular problems of learning experienced by students in the classrooms, confirming the nature of a problem, and evaluating the impact of interventions.

Peer coaching plays a potentially crucial role in enhancing the impact of interventions created to solve problems of student learning (Costa & Garmston, 1994; Joyce & Showers, 1988). Peer coaching provides a framework for teachers to help one another improve instruction. The improvement process involves data gathering, observation, and feeding back information requested by a colleague engaged in the act of teaching.

Considered alone, each component appears to exert a positive influence on teacher behavior and on student learning. Taken together, the effects of each component are enhanced. This chapter is centered on descriptions of our experiences with each of the components, as well as findings in the literature regarding the impact of collaborative inquiry on teacher behavior and student learning. We conclude with some suggestions about combining the components to increase the use of creative intelligence by teacher-leaders.

Collaborative Inquiry

One hallmark of any profession is skilled inquiry that determines the effectiveness of the profession. Conducting such inquiry may be accomplished by lone practitioners or by groups of practitioners. Teachers working with other educators and citizens to inquire into the effects of their practice may accomplish more together than alone. Although some benefits of collaborative inquiry exist in individual teacher inquiry, participation with others taps the social nature of the construction of knowledge and the collective nature of knowing (e.g., Rogoff & Lave, 1984; Vygotsky, 1986). Group participation creates opportunities for learning, increases the resources available to individuals, and enables teachers to process shared information through communication and collaboration (Rosenholtz, 1989). Because much of teacher knowledge is tacit and based on experience (Kagan, 1990), teachers acting alone may experience difficulty in articulating assumptions, beliefs, and understandings in ways necessary for conscious examination. As individuals interact in groups, they are likely to acquire common understandings and language. Group discussion becomes a vehicle for articulating, examining, and changing teacher beliefs (Schecter & Parkhurst, 1993). In turn, teacher beliefs strongly influence behavior (Bandura, 1986). Although beliefs are traditionally resistant to change, some evidence exists that the combination of collaboration and reflection over a period of years affects teacher beliefs and teaching practices (Hunsaker & Johnston, 1992). On the other hand, traditional staff development has little success in effecting lasting change, perhaps because teachers seldom experience a clear link between their needs and the in-service opportunities provided (Anders & Richardson, 1994; Fullan, 1990).

Teacher involvement in collaborative inquiry with other teachers or university-based researchers provides several benefits. Participation in inquiry teams holds promise for solving instructional problems and for creating a school culture supportive of teacher reflection and experimentation (Francis, Hirsch, & Rowland, 1994). Previous researchers on teacher participation in action research and collaboration for school improvement report professional and personal growth for teachers (Goswami & Stillman, 1987; Maloy & Jones, 1987; Oja & Pine, 1987). In general, collaborative inquiry provides a means of increasing the likelihood that teachers will apply the results of research in their classrooms. This use of results by teachers reduces the time lag between inquiry and application, introduces the complexity of the classroom to research studies (Tikunoff & Ward, 1983), and permits the pooling of university and school expertise and resources to transform schools (Lieberman, 1992).

Through collaborative inquiry, teachers perceive a heightened sense of professional community and reduced feelings of isolation in the workplace (Goswami & Stillman, 1987; Maloy & Jones, 1987; Oja & Pine, 1987). In this way, collaboration serves as an intrinsic reward to build commitment to teaching (Firestone & Pennell, 1993). With increased opportunities for learning, teachers recognize that others share similar problems. Engagement in joint activities to directly address these problems in helping children receive a high-quality education may also increase teachers' feelings of professional efficacy.

Collaboration between university and teacher researchers, in particular, eases school-university tensions created by the gap between the worlds of research and practice and provides meaningful staff development for university faculty, teachers, and administrators (Knight, Wiseman, & Smith, 1993). Furthermore, the close association of university and teacher researchers should result in research that is clearly related to concerns of teachers who work daily in the reality of classrooms. This leads to better understanding and increased utilization of research by classroom teachers. Educational researchers often address problems they can answer rather than investigate the more complex issues associated with schooling that practitioners must face (Cuban, 1992). Traditionally, when educational research is used to address theoretical as opposed to concrete problems, it does not result in direct impact on practice (see, e.g., Finn, 1988). On the other hand, local knowledge of the type typically generated by practitioners is often incomplete and insular (Goldenberg & Gallimore, 1991). The fusion of research findings and local knowledge generated as a result of collaboration of teachers and university researchers may provide results more directly applicable to practitioners' concerns. In short, collaborative inquiry promises to strengthen needed links between theory and practice.

Study Teams

The teacher study team is a powerful way to explore and solve problems blocking student learning. The steps displayed in Figure 4.2 represent the components of the study team process used in a number of elementary, middle, and high schools across the country. Study teams are conducted in individual schools, districtwide, and nationally. Most examples cited here occurred in individual schools. These study teams may focus on a problem affecting the entire school, a particular grade level, a special department, a specific subject, a single student, or some combination.

The study team process typically begins with spirited dialogue exploring various problems inhibiting student learning. The process then turns to discovery of the most important problem to which the study team members wish to devote their attention. Teachers elaborate their definition of the problem and confirm its nature and importance. The study team fashions actions designed to solve the problem. Finally, the study team evaluates the impact of those actions on the learning of children. This summative evaluation leads to renewed dialogue. Throughout the process, formative evaluation of each step of the process occurs, leading to adjustments as deliberations advance.

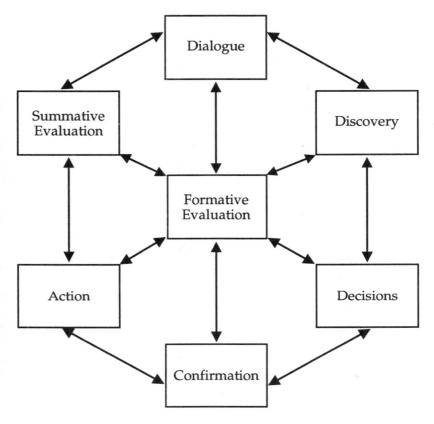

Figure 4.2. The National Coalition Study Team Process

The study teams following this process typically consist of 5 to 25 volunteer members of a school faculty who meet together to work on issues of mutual concern. Beyond the general process employed, the nature of the teams and the specific implementation procedures used differ greatly. Although some campuses use only one study team, other schools report as many as five study teams operating simultaneously on different concerns. A number of teams discuss individual students, devise procedures to use with these learners, try those procedures, and examine their impact. These "case study teams" differ from study teams that work with organizational and programmatic issues or study a combination of individual student and organizational issues. Some teams are drawn from the entire faculty, whereas other teams may represent only one grade level or subject. Many teams meet regularly for extended periods of time; other teams meet periodically to complete the study team cycle of activities. Alternatively, teams may gather only three or four times to investigate an issue and develop solutions, leaving for others the evaluation of results. A number of teams enlist as a regular member an "expert" resource, such as a professor or a central office staff member, from outside the school. Other teams call on experts only from time to time or rely on their own resources. In a few cases, teams link their work with projects conducted by teachers as researchers. In other cases, teams use teacher research strategies as the primary intervention for a commonly shared problem.

Based on study team experiences recorded in one school district, three types of findings about their operation and impact emerged. First are the lessons originally taught by Ralph Tyler (1992) about the ability of teachers to apply their creative intelligence to solutions of instructional problems. Next are findings of research in one local district about the relationship between study team participation and teacher improvement. Finally, a number of operating principles emerging from the experiences of teachers and administrators working with study teams are reported (see Table 4.1).

The Tyler Lessons

Outcomes reported from study team efforts across the member schools working nationally to improve student learning (Ghory, 1994) suggest that teachers, parents, and principals are capable of identifying and framing solutions to persistent learning problems experienced by their students. Collaborative inquiry, as an approach to developing solutions to learning problems, represents a departure for many teachers and principals. Reliance on packaged programs developed by experts outside the local school is a typical way of addressing problems in schools and school districts. This apparent infatuation with implementing the "newest solution of choice" mirrors the expectation of large numbers of teachers that they and their colleagues need to rely on the prescriptions of putative outside experts rather than on their own professional judgments. The teachers we work with reject this idea.

Results of the study team process (Ghory, 1994; Smith, 1995, 1996) suggest that large numbers of children in a variety of locations became more successful in learning after receiving interventions designed by school study teams rather than by the application of prescribed approaches. These changes included increases in measured reading comprehension, increases in writing performance, increases in the amount of reading completed, improvements in English language proficiency, greater fluency and clarity in oral language, decreases in special education referrals, improved grades, fewer disciplinary incidents, and enhanced problem-solving behaviors.

These improvements also suggest that focusing on the individual problems experienced by students pays off in student learning and organizational change. In addition to reporting improvements in student performance, a number of schools reported other kinds of procedural and policy changes. For example, a few schools reported major changes in the teaching of reading based on study team deliberations. At least two schools, as part of their study team actions, changed the way in which students were grouped for instruction. Many schools reported a diminution in the tendency to label students and a heightened propensity among faculty to focus on the learning problems of individual students.

This focus on individual students signals one aspect of change in school climate that appears to be associated with the use of study teams (Francis et al., 1994). Many principals and teachers reported the development of a climate in which faculties take pride in their ability to identify and solve problems individuals experience in their learning (Smith, 1994). Initial successes with study teams appear to lead to the creation of multiple study teams and the adoption of new modes of problem solving in school organizations. For example, two schools took off in different directions with their first study teams: One school focused on programmatic issues, and the other employed a case study approach to understanding learning problems. After the second year of operation, exchange visits by teachers resulted in additional case study and programmatic study teams operating on both campuses. In an increasing number of schools, addressing problems in learning through the use of study teams has become the norm, suggesting that schools are moving toward what some management scholars call a "learning organization" (Senge, 1990).

None of these changes resulted from the mass implementation of new programs. Rather, they came from the hard work necessary to make desired changes in local school environments, designed to address carefully identified learning problems, accomplished teacher by teacher and student by student. This observation suggests that meaningful and lasting change is incremental and directed toward particular problems.

TABLE 4.1. Lessons Learned From the Study Team Process

- Teachers, parents, and principals are capable of identifying and framing solutions to the most persistent learning problems experienced by their students.

- Focusing on the individual learning problems experienced by students pays off in student and organizational learning.

- Meaningful and lasting change is incremental.

- Participation in study team problem-solving is associated with positive teacher perceptions regarding student achievement and teaching behavior.

- It takes time for staff to conceptualize priorities based on a diagnosis of the problems of learning to be addressed.

- Solving problems of learning is much more difficult but more rewarding than "doing programs."

- Case study teams are strengthened by collective behaviors of suspended judgment, accurate identification of learning problems, and the crafting of solutions proximate to the problems of learning identified.

- Progress is more difficult to achieve in secondary than in elementary schools and in high schools than in middle schools.

- The weakest links in the study team process are the confirmation or verification of problems and the evaluations of actions.

Findings About Teacher Improvement

Changes in organizational behavior do not occur without changes in the reasoning and practices of individuals inhabiting the organization (Argyris, 1982). Research conducted in one local school district assessed the impact of study team participation on teachers' perceptions of professional development and student learning. Initial findings suggest that the positive perceptions associated with study team membership may increase with the amount and extent of participation in study teams (Knight & Smith, 1995). The research found clear and significant differences between study team participants ($N = 244$) and nonparticipants ($N = 100$) in their responses to survey item scales measuring satisfaction with teaching, professional interest, and sense of ability to influence learning. Despite the fact that all respondents displayed positive responses, study team participants exhibited significantly higher satisfaction, greater professional interest, and a greater sense of effectiveness in improving student learning. These findings represent no surprise, however, because it would be expected that teachers who volunteer to join study teams would display such perceptions to a greater degree than teachers who choose not to become involved. Nevertheless, the association between these perceptions and study team membership suggests that study teams may represent an important avenue for professional growth and development.

This suggestion gains credence from an analysis of perceptions among study team participants. The variable associated with the greatest difference in perceptions appears to be the number of years of involvement in study teams, with more years of involvement generally associated with higher degrees of professional interest and a greater sense of impact on student achievement, attitudes, and behaviors. Additionally, teachers with more years of experience with study teams were more likely to indicate changes in their teaching behaviors as a result of study team participation (e.g., using new teaching, assessment, and diagnostic techniques and using a greater variety of techniques).

Analyses of the relationship of years of teaching experience and educational level with teacher perceptions revealed an unexpected finding. Teachers with fewer years of experience were more likely than teachers with more experience to perceive positive study team impact on student attendance and homework completion, whereas teachers with less education were more likely than teachers with more education to believe that study teams influence student attitudes and behaviors. It may be that teachers with less experience and education have fewer techniques to influence student learning and thus are more likely to acquire new strategies from study teams. This explanation seemed to be the preferred interpretation by teachers interviewed in postsurvey focus groups.

Taken together, these findings suggest that study teams can provide an important avenue for teacher growth. With increasing involvement in study teams, teachers try on more new behavior and see greater impact on student learning. Finally, it is promising that teachers with less experience and education may benefit the most from participation in study teams.

Findings About Conducting Study Teams

As schools experiment with study teams, a number of observations about conducting study teams are reported. Drawn from a variety of discussions in study teams, a series of meetings among elementary assistant principals related to conducting case study teams, and informal conversations with teachers and principals, these observations appear to be widely shared. To begin, it takes time for staff to conceptualize priorities based on a diagnosis of learning problems. It is surely easier to apply packaged educational solutions across classrooms and schools, regardless of their relation to the actual problems students experience in those settings. The extra time that it takes to untangle problems and create solutions tends to make the process more difficult. At first, study teams can be perceived as "just one more thing" added to the pressures and constraints surrounding the job of the teacher. Only when it becomes clear that the study team approach benefits students and helps teachers does the work become a normal part of effective leadership rather than an additional chore. At that point, the consensus appears to be that solving problems of learning is much more difficult, but more rewarding, than "doing programs."

When elementary assistant principals in one local school district gathered to discuss their experience with study teams, they made the following suggestions:

- Identify the child's learning strengths. Determine what he or she is able to do well. Study team participants learn that it is helpful to begin with an assessment of what the child is able to do rather than operate with the perspective of eliminating a deficit. Perseverance on deficits excludes approaches to learning that build on strengths. Insistence on mastery of deficits, moreover, appears to impede other learning of which the child may be capable (Slavin, 1987). When the team considers learning strengths, more often than not a successful solution can be framed that takes advantage of what the child can do and allows the child to extend learning, despite learning deficits.

■ Consider the individual child's learning progress without comparison to that of his or her peers. Associated with approaching problems of learning from an analysis of weaknesses is a tendency to define a child's weaknesses primarily in relation to other children's strengths. A more useful comparison may be found by noting progress of individuals against their own starting points, based on an assessment of what they did do rather than on what they did not do.

■ Spend less time on why the problem exists and more time on describing the problem accurately. Members of some study teams experience difficulty in making progress on developing solutions when the conversation turns to limning out the reasons for the problems children experience (e.g., family dysfunction, social disorganization, conditions of poverty, low motivation, poor behavior). These discussions may encourage avoidance of responsibility on the part of educators and lead to lower expectations for student performance. Solutions tend to be found more quickly and more appropriately when the conversation emphasizes the nature of the problem, the ways in which it appears, and the confirmation of its existence.

■ Share a belief that the student can make progress in learning. Study team participants express strong conviction that unless the teachers share a belief that all students can make progress, the solutions will not work.

■ Enrich the study team conversation by excluding labels and centering on the child's specific learning behaviors. Members of study teams report that discussing children and their problems through general characterizations such as "learning disabled," "gifted learner," or "attention deficit" tends to be a nonproductive practice. When the discussion leaves the labels out and concentrates on specific learning behaviors, progress quickens.

- Emphasize what can be done to engender success for the child rather than lower expectations for learning. Some study teams have a tendency to respond immediately to a problem of learning difficulty by lowering the expected level of learning attainment. Participants of successful study teams report a more productive procedure of holding constant the level of expectation and varying the instructional procedure.

- Suspend judgment about a child's situation as understanding of the learning problem emerges. Successful study teams tend to reach an understanding of the problem to be addressed before rushing to judgment on interventions designed to help the child.

- Determine what can be done to help a child rather than just deciding who will help the child. A number of teams report that one form of rushing to judgment occurs when the team decides to match a student with an older peer or a "teacher buddy" without any clear idea of how such a match would treat the problem the student experiences. Participants of successful teams learn that a more effective response resides in determining the nature of the intervention required before selecting the person or persons to help the child.

- Consider individual solutions, such as revising instructional strategies, rather than relying on solutions that are organizational in nature. Matching students with organizational solutions, such as retention or referral to special education, represents a fairly typical unproductive response of study teams in the beginning stages of operation. Such organizational solutions generally are reached in the absence of specific problem definition. Successful teams find developing individual instructional solutions that relate to the problem diagnosis a more effective procedure.

- Fashion instructional solutions proximate to the specific problem. For example, teach the child how to look for context clues if the child does not do so rather than alter the entire approach to reading instruction or merely change the text the child will read. Similarly, if a child displays difficulty in performing subtraction because of failure to understand the concept of subtraction, it is not sufficient to find additional problems on which the child may practice. Instead, a study team interested in finding proximate solutions may recommend that the child be shown how to use concrete materials, such as blocks, to foster understanding of the concept of subtraction prior to performing subtraction with abstract symbols.

■ Evaluate the effectiveness of solutions. Effective study teams spend time following up on the success of the solutions and keep track of the progress displayed by all children considered.

Taken together, these suggestions for conducting case study teams will be strengthened through collective behaviors of suspending judgment, accurately identifying learning problems, and crafting solutions proximate to the learning problems. Learning these and other strategies for successful study teams appears to occur earlier, more readily, and more often in elementary schools than in middle schools, and in middle schools compared to high schools. Few question this conclusion. Less clear is why secondary schools inhibit collaborative inquiry and what to do about it. Teacher perceptions tend to refute the contentions often heard that secondary school teachers' content orientation leads them to care less or do less about individual problems of student learning. No significant differences appeared between secondary and elementary school teachers' perceptions of the impact of study teams on teacher behaviors or student learning (Knight & Smith, 1995).

Siskin (1995) argues that educational reformers and students of educational change give too little notice to the importance of academic departments in secondary schools and that productive work should take into account the defining role and power of these academic departments. Concerned about this difference in study team success among school levels and aware of the importance of academic departments, high school administrators and teachers in a local school district began to organize study teams focusing on particular problems students experience in learning a specific subject. Additionally, two university professors conducted a teacher research project across two high schools that also involved the use of study teams sensitive to problems students were experiencing in subjects. Initial results appear promising. Despite what may be greater difficulties with implementation in secondary schools, the study team process appears to be taking hold. Although considerable progress is occurring, the weakest links in the study team process are the verification of problems and the evaluation of solutions. Work on enhancing the evaluation process so that these weaknesses can be corrected takes a number of forms, including participation in district and national study teams devoted to evaluation and local efforts designed to encourage teacher research.

Teacher Research

Teacher research, as typically described in the literature (Cochran-Smith & Lytle, 1990; Patterson et al., 1990), complements the study team process and is particularly well suited to the tasks of identifying and verifying learning problems and evaluating actions taken to solve learning problems. Teachers identify their students' problems, develop their own research questions, conduct their own investigations, and derive their own solutions. Although a number of teachers have conducted impressive classroom research (e.g., Feagins, 1995) connected to study team efforts, the connections between these forms of inquiry need future study. Notions about what constitutes teacher research vary considerably (see, e.g., Clift, Houston, & Pugach, 1990; Hollingsworth & Sockett, 1994; Schön, 1983). Inquiry assumes different forms and serves different purposes depending on the perspective and purpose of the researcher.

One useful approach to the conceptualization of teacher research separates "practical inquiry" from "formal research" (Richardson, 1994, p. 7). Formal research uses traditional methodologies, applies criteria for judging its own quality or rigor, and seeks to add to the formal knowledge base about teaching. Although teachers may engage in formal research, many of them prefer to pursue practical inquiry as it usually results in immediate transfer to the classroom. Nevertheless, both types of inquiry contribute in different ways to knowledge of teaching and learning (Hargreaves, 1996).

Practical inquiry, more difficult to define and currently less pre-scriptive than formal research, may be viewed as existing on a continuum in which the research procedures range from highly systematic to loosely structured. Viewed from one end of the contin-uum, the act of teaching is an informal way of "doing research." Teachers, in the course of their work, constantly try new strategies or new curricula, observe the impact of the intervention, and decide whether the intervention worked or not. A danger of this approach lies in the possibility that teachers may judge what works without consciously examining the assumptions and beliefs underlying their judgments (Richardson, 1994).

Another conceptualization of practical inquiry casts the teacher in the role of reflective practitioner (Schön, 1983). However, reflection is more structured than typical teaching permits. In this approach, conscious application of the scientific method to teaching creates a framework that cues reflection. Teachers identify problems, study the problems through active engagement in classroom problem-solving, and reach conclusions. A critical step in this type of reflective practice is the suspension of judgment about solutions until teachers establish the parameters of the problem and collect and interpret data.

The most systematic version of reflective practice is what we refer to as "teacher research." But the difference between teacher research and formal research becomes less delineated as teachers design and implement more rigorous qualitative and quantitative studies and publish their findings (see, e.g., Patterson et al., 1990). Teacher research becomes a powerful means of improving practice and enhancing understanding of learning problems. It often brings increased resources to bear on these persistent educational problems. The quality of teacher research is defined in terms of the utility of the results. Viewing teacher and formal research from this pragmatic perspective suggests a less rigid differentiation between the two approaches (see, e.g., Hargreaves, 1996) and legitimizes teacher contributions to the systematic inquiry into crucial problems in education.

Peer Coaching

Consideration of peer coaching completes an effective conception of collaborative inquiry. The literature about peer coaching indicates that teachers who engage in it can improve their instructional behaviors and exert a positive impact on student learning (Joyce & Showers, 1988; Sparks, 1986; Sparks & Loucks-Horsley, 1990). A variety of approaches to peer coaching exist, ranging from highly structured teaching pairs helping one another implement an instructional procedure (Joyce & Showers, 1988) to flexible clinical supervision (Goldhammer, 1966; Goldhammer, Anderson, & Krajewski, 1980) and cognitive coaching (Costa & Garmston, 1985, 1994).

The peer coaching described here shares three common criteria. First, the teacher being coached is in control of what is to be observed and how the observation is to be conducted. Second, the coach is obligated to provide feedback from the observation to his or her colleagues. Finally, the feedback must not add data beyond the original agreement about what was to be observed.

Despite the recent rejection of the claimed benefits of peer feedback by Showers and Joyce (1996), the positive effects of objective mirroring of teacher behaviors have been amply demonstrated (Sparks & Loucks-Horsley, 1990). The position taken by Showers and Joyce appears to be based on their expressed belief that teachers are unable to give objective feedback and cannot resist evaluative remarks. They provide no data other than anecdotal reports from teachers to support their stance. This argument seems to devalue the professional behaviors of teachers and contradicts our experiences with teachers engaged in peer coaching.

Peers can coach one another to implement desired changes in teacher behavior, reflect on why particular instructional decisions were made or should be made, or hone a particular instructional skill. We suggest that peer coaching directed toward improving instruction in the service of solving problems of student learning will be more effective in promoting student achievement than peer coaching directed toward implementing prescribed procedures or perfecting isolated, discrete skills. Furthermore, we argue that the impact of peer coaching on student learning is increased when informed by accurate descriptions of problems and careful assessments of particular instructional interventions that can arise from participation in teacher research and study teams.

Combining the Three Components
of Collaborative Inquiry

Used separately, each component of collaborative inquiry—study teams, teacher research, and peer coaching—appears to improve teacher effectiveness and increase student learning. We suggest that the impact of any component may be strengthened by combining it with one or both of the other components of collaborative inquiry. For example, in conjunction with study team participation, teachers also may choose to engage in more systematic teacher research, individually or with school or university colleagues, to further investigate specific aspects of learning problems associated with study team topics. In addition, teachers also may elect to work with other teachers in peer coaching dyads to collect and interpret data about the improvement of instructional practices related to learning problems being considered by study teams. Combining study teams with teacher research and peer coaching provides teachers with opportunities to engage in various kinds of inquiry and to pursue group as well as individual priorities for learning. In this manner, teachers practice instructional leadership designed to improve teaching and learning in classrooms.

Another example of combining the three components provides some early evidence for the effectiveness of this conception of collaborative inquiry (see Boudah & Knight, 1996). Study teams of high school teachers working with university professors determined that students who were not achieving well lacked strategies for learning. The educators developed an intervention, coached one another on its implementation, and researched its effects on students and teachers. They found that students receiving intervention made progress in solving their learning problems. Teachers became more confident about working with low-achieving students, changed the way they interacted with these students, and expressed more positive attitudes about teaching them. Here, the study team anchors the collaborative inquiry by providing a means to explore problems and solutions, design related teacher research studies, form peer coaching dyads, and eventually discuss findings. Even teachers who do not conduct teacher research or engage in peer coaching benefit from the reports of those who participate in these activities. However, teachers who engage in all three components of collaborative inquiry will likely benefit most.

Closing

Collaborative inquiry, defined as study teams, teacher research, and peer coaching working together, is an effective way to solve problems of student learning. When teachers work closely with one another in formal and informal ways and look carefully at how their students are progressing, they refine their teaching and adjust their curriculum so that more students who live and learn in adverse circumstances benefit from their school environments. In particular, we note changes in teacher thinking, improvements in instructional behavior, and reforms in school culture resulting from collaboration. Taken together, the three components of collaborative inquiry promote the practice of creative intelligence by teachers, placing them in leadership roles for the identification and creative solution of problems of student learning.

References

Anders, P., & Richardson, V. (1994). Launching a new form of staff development. In V. Richardson (Ed.), *Teacher change and staff development process* (pp. 1-22). New York: Teachers College Press.

Argyris, C. (1982). *Reasoning, learning and action: Individual and organizational.* San Francisco: Jossey-Bass.

Bandura, A. (1986). *Social foundations of thought and action: A social cognitive theory.* Englewood Cliffs, NJ: Prentice Hall.

Boudah, D., & Knight, S. (1996, June). *Beyond bridging the gap: Creating learning communities of research and practice.* (Grant report submitted to the Office of Special Education Programs)

Clift, R., Houston, R., & Pugach, M. (1990). *Encouraging reflective practice in education: An analysis of issues and programs.* New York: Teachers College Press.

Cochran-Smith, M., & Lytle, S. (1990). Research on teaching and teacher research: The issues that divide. *Educational Researcher, 19*, 2-11.

Costa, A., & Garmston, R. (1985). Supervision for intelligent teaching. *Educational Leadership, 42*(5), 70-80.

Costa, A., & Garmston, R. (1994). *Cognitive coaching: Approaching renaissance schools.* Norwood, MA: Christopher Gordon.

Cuban, L. (1992). Managing educational dilemmas. *Educational Researcher, 21*, 4-11.

Dewey, J. (1933). *How we think: A restatement of the relation of reflective thinking to the educative process.* Boston: Heath.

Feagins, H. (1995). Using structured questions to improve self evaluation of writing. *Texas Reading Report, 16*, 5-7.

Finn, C. (1988). What ails education research? *Educational Researcher, 17*, 5-8.

Firestone, W., & Pennell, J. (1993). Teacher commitment, working conditions, and differential incentive policies. *Review of Educational Research, 63*, 489-525.

Francis, S., Hirsch, S., & Rowland, E. (1994). Improving school culture through study groups. *Journal of Staff Development, 13*, 12-15.

Fullan, M. (1990). Staff development, innovation, and institutional development. In B. Joyce (Ed.), *Changing school culture through staff development* (pp. 3-25). Alexandria, VA: ASCD.

Ghory, W. J. (1994). *National Coalition for Equality in Learning: Year four evaluation report.* Unpublished manuscript, Amherst, MA.

Goldenberg, C., & Gallimore, C. (1991). Local knowledge, research knowledge and educational change: A case study of early Spanish reading improvement. *Educational Researcher, 20*, 6-14.

Goldhammer, R. (1966). *Clinical supervision: Special methods for the supervision of teachers.* New York: Holt, Rinehart & Winston.

Goldhammer, R., Anderson, R., & Krajewski, R. (1980). *Clinical supervision.* New York: Holt, Rinehart & Winston.

Goswami, D., & Stillman, P. (1987). *Reclaiming the classroom: Teacher research as an agency for change.* Upper Montclair, NJ: Boynton Cook.

Hargreaves, A. (1996). Transforming knowledge: Blurring the boundaries between research, policy, and practice. *Educational Evaluation and Policy Analysis, 18*(2), 105-122.

Hollingsworth, S., & Sockett, H. (1994). *Teacher research and educational reform* (NSSE Yearbook). Chicago: University of Chicago Press.

Hunsaker, L., & Johnston, M. (1992). Teacher under construction: A collaborative study of teacher change. *American Educational Research Journal, 29*, 350-372.

Joyce, B., & Showers, B. (1988). *Student achievement through staff development.* White Plains, NY: Longman.

Kagan, D. (1990). Goldilocks principle. *Review of Educational Research, 60*(3), 419-469.

Knight, S., & Smith, R. G. (1995, April). *Examining the effects of teacher inquiry on teacher perceptions and cognitions.* Paper presented at the American Educational Research Association Meeting, San Francisco.

Knight, S., Wiseman, D., & Smith, C. (1993). The reflectivity-activity dilemma in school-university partnerships. *Journal of Teacher Education, 43*, 269-277.

Lieberman, A. (1992). The meaning of scholarly activity and the building of community. *Educational Researcher, 21,* 5-12.

Maloy, R., & Jones, B. (1987). Teachers, partnerships, and school improvement. *Journal of Research and Development, 20,* 19-24.

Oja, S., & Pine, G. (1987). Collaborative action research: Teachers' stages of development and school context. *Peabody Journal of Education, 64,* 96-116.

Patterson, L., Stansell, J., & Lee, S. (1990). *Teacher research: From promise to power.* Katonah, NY: Richard C. Owen.

Richardson, V. (1994), Conducting research on practice. *Educational Researcher, 23,* 5-10.

Rogoff, B., & Lave, J. (1984). *Everyday cognition.* Cambridge, MA: Harvard University Press.

Rosenholtz, S. (1989). *Teachers' workplace: The social organization of schools.* New York: Longman.

Schecter, S., & Parkhurst, S. (1993). Ideological divergences in a teacher-research group. *American Educational Research Journal, 30,* 771-798.

Schön, D. (1983). *The reflective practitioner.* New York: Basic Books.

Senge, P. M. (1990). *The fifth discipline: The art and practice of the learning organization.* New York: Doubleday.

Showers, B., & Joyce, B. (1996). The evolution of peer coaching. *Educational Leadership, 53*(6), 12-16.

Sinclair, R. (1992, October). *The National Coalition problem solving process.* Workshop presentation, National Coalition for Equality in Education Facilitators and Superintendents Meeting, Vail, CO.

Siskin, L. S. (1995). *Realms of knowledge: Academic departments in secondary schools.* Washington, DC: Falmer.

Slavin, R. E. (1987). Mastery learning reconsidered. *Review of Educational Research, 57,* 175-213.

Smith, R. G. (1994). Teacher study teams: A focused approach to school problem solving. *ERS Spectrum, 12*(3), 13-19.

Smith, R. G. (1995). *Spring Independent School District evaluation report: Facilitator summary.* Unpublished manuscript, Spring Independent School District, Houston, TX.

Smith, R. G. (1996). Fashioning effective solutions: The promise of school study teams. *Equity and Excellence in Education, 29*(1), 20-29.

Sparks, D., & Loucks-Horsley, S. (1990). Models of staff development. In W. R. Houston (Ed.), *Handbook of research on teacher education* (pp. 234-250). New York: Macmillan.

Sparks, G. (1986). The effectiveness of alternative training activities in changing teaching practices. *American Educational Research Journal, 23,* 217-225.

Tikunoff, W., & Ward, B. (1983). Collaborative research on teaching. *Elementary School Journal, 83,* 453-468.

Tyler, R. W. (1992). *Improving school effectiveness.* Amherst, MA: National Coalition for Equality in Learning.

Vygotsky, L. (1986). *Thought and language* (A. Kozulin, Trans.). Cambridge, MA: MIT Press.

Learning From Families 5

HOPE JENSEN LEICHTER

In attempting to improve cooperation between families and schools and to enhance the contributions of families to their children's education, those of us working with the National Coalition for Equality in Learning are discovering that it is possible to achieve a more nuanced understanding of families, their educational possibilities, and their relationships with schools. Achieving a new mode of understanding is particularly important because perceptions of families, especially other people's families, are too often locked in a veil of stereotypes ranging from subtle to blatant. Indeed, stereotypes inhere in the language used to label families in terms of such features as ethnicity and family structure. Teachers and family members know one another mainly in terms of particular parts of their lives—an example of the segmental vision that pervades complex societies. The basic issue is how those adults closest to children can extend their vision of one another's lives and work to find even more productive points of contact between home and school.

Communicating Through Stories

Family stories and family memories offer one vehicle for changing the lens through which families are seen.[1] The realization that stories are fundamental modes of communication may be found, among other places, in a classic analysis by Gregory Bateson (1979). He argues that stories are basic to all cognition and uses a story about a man and his computer as an illustration. In an effort to understand how the mind works, the man asks his computer how it thinks. After a pause for analysis, the computer prints out its answer: "That reminds me of a story."

From this illustration, Bateson (1979) goes on to argue that stories are fundamental to all cognition, in all forms of life, from the sea anemone to the redwood forest.

Stories are not merely anecdotes. On the contrary, stories are the basic form in which all communications take place. What is more, stories are a fundamental mode in which ideas are handed down from one generation to another, often embellished and modified. Thus, stories are one of the modes in which memories are stored and retrieved. A key in Bateson's illustration is the phrase *that reminds me of*. Stories are evocative, they have the power to trigger and remind us of other stories, in part because of their details, and in this respect, they are basic forms of linkage.

In fact, one of the most compelling things that we have learned through encouraging school administrators, teachers, and family members to discuss their family stories and family memories is the significance of *that reminds me of*. The power of stories to trigger the recollection of other stories is vital in their potential to touch the heart and create a basis for empathy. Not all stories are appreciated by everyone, and the triggering mechanisms may be indirect. Because stories are often connected through analogy, the parts of one story that trigger recollections of another story are not necessarily predictable. But this is one reason stories allow discovery.

The term *story* has an everyday ring that may make it seem insignificant and not part of a serious, scientific examination of education. But the field of sophisticated analysis of narratives is extensive, as Jerome Bruner points out in, among other writings, *Acts of Meaning* (1990). The literature on narratives offers further ideas about subtle ways in which the use of story or narrative forms may be applied to educational practice, and indeed, a growing number of educational scholars are making use of stories, for example, as vehicles for understanding teacher roles (Dyson & Genishi, 1994; Paley, 1981). In considering the characteristics of narratives, Bruner notes that they are inherently sequential and that they are neutral with respect to reality status—good stories are not necessarily true stories—but this does not detract from their significance. What is more, built into good narratives or good stories is what some call trouble, in that they derive their excitement or charge from problems and solutions to problems or violations of cultural canons and ways of making things right again. A key point is that narratives contain a dual focus, both on descriptions of actions and events and on the narrators' subjective reactions to these actions and events. In this respect, narratives are a way of interpreting the world and a clue to how others see it. Their complexity and subtlety offer educators a powerful tool for helping to understand families. Listening to and reflecting on family stories helped us to understand what needs to be done so that families and schools may join more effectively to improve the learning of children who live and learn in both places.

Seeking to Improve Collaboration

Recommendations for increasing the cooperation between families and schools and the involvement of parents in their children's education abound in educational discussions today. And there are good reasons for these recommendations. The numerous problems that interfere with children's learning cannot be corrected by schools alone. It has long been recognized that families are always educators of their children and that the success of schooling depends to a significant degree on the contributions of the home (Leichter, 1974, 1979). In a recent issue of *Daedalus*, "American Schools: Still Separate, Still Unequal" (1995), a number of scholars reemphasize the need for family and community involvement if the educational reforms that would reduce inequalities are to succeed. As Harold Howe (1995) notes, "the impact of destructive environments on the everyday lives of children cannot be overcome in classrooms alone. The social interventions aimed at reducing the effects of these pervasive forces will have to bring schools, families, and communities together on a planned basis" (p. 72). Patricia Albjerg Graham (1995) sums up the point, contending that "action must come from families and communities" (p. 46).

If one accepts the view that the problems with children's learning involve far more than schooling, dilemmas arise regarding what role schools can have in initiating corrections to problems originating elsewhere. Yet, schools are one logical place to begin such efforts, as they have daily responsibility for children. One reasonable starting point is to improve communications between home and school, not just to address problems arising outside the school, but also to find supports from families and communities for children's learning.

Here, a further dilemma arises about how to understand the families from which schoolchildren come. Unfortunately, formulations of the need for parent involvement with children's schooling sometimes rest on *tabula rasa* assumptions about families, implying that without the intervention of the school, parents would not be involved with their children's education or have adequate ideas about child rearing. These assumptions are reflected in the litanies one hears about parents who presumably are not concerned with their children's schooling or competent enough to bring up their children. In the *tabula rasa* view, it is often forgotten that many forms of family involvement in the education of children and many forms of communication between families and schools already exist. It is forgotten that children go daily between home and school, bringing home reports about school and going to school with reports about home. It is forgotten that parents, grandparents, and other relatives have distinct memories of their own personal experiences with schooling. It is forgotten that parents are exposed to issues about schooling via the media, in which discussion of such topics as the failure of children on reading and math tests, schools taxes, emergencies in school buildings, disciplinary problems, and crimes in schools are common. It is forgotten that questions of educational policy and practice are frequent subjects of public political debate and public decision making in national and local elections. It is forgotten that parents, whatever their level of schooling, are exposed to ideas about the formal education that is required for various careers. Finally, it is forgotten that not only ideas about schooling but ideas about child development, child rearing, and the family's role in education also come to parents from a variety of sources, including their relatives, friends, neighbors, clergy, and religious texts, as well as the media.

Relying on the Creative Intelligence of Families

We have a different view about families and learning. All parents are involved in their children's education, and all families are capable of making significant contributions to their children's learning. We start by recognizing the many forms of involvement that families already have as fundamental educators of their children—the kinds of points that are often forgotten—and seek ways to build upon their contributions. A corollary premise is that schooling is only one important source of education. Significant education also occurs in families and communities. It is not just a question of families supporting the education that takes place in schools but also of schools supporting lifelong education in families and communities.

A related premise concerns the aim of improving the learning of all children. Our work across the country was founded with the goal of finding ways of reducing the inequalities that are associated with poverty—the kinds of conditions that Jonathan Kozol (1991) described so movingly in *Savage Inequalities*. We recognize full well that problems of educational achievement are disproportionately associated with economic poverty and minority status, but we believe that the problems of equality in learning must be attended to by addressing the difficulties that inhibit the learning of all children. We are concerned with reducing the discrimination that limits the opportunities of those from economic poverty and minority status. We are also concerned with reducing the detrimental effects of moral poverty—the fear and prejudice that prevent adults and children from examining and empathizing with the conditions of others.

Another premise that guides our action concerns the importance of what John Dewey and others have called "creative intelligence." The idea here is that solutions to complex problems can be found by the exercise of creative intelligence on the part of all those involved in the problems. This applies to families and children, teachers and other school personnel, and members of the community. The belief in the creative intelligence of all participants in social situations is quintessentially optimistic and democratic, though characteristically not always easy to maintain. Yet, this ideal is not merely an empty platitude; it has distinct implications for the role of educator.

We are sometimes asked if these premises apply to so-called dysfunctional families. The answer is that without trivializing the pain of families beset with multiple problems or naively romanticizing the strengths of families we recognize that all families are dysfunctional in some ways at some times—surely this is revealed by introspection—and that even families that are overwhelmed with the most serious troubles have moments of overcoming their problems and ways of being functional. At the very least, we believe it is more helpful to err on the side of assuming a family has capacities for overcoming difficulties and to search for these capacities than to foreclose such a search by applying negative labels that imply that the problem lies in essential characteristics of the family and therefore cannot be modified.

Choreographing Discovery

If one relies on the creative intelligence of all participants, the basic task of the educator becomes assisting in the process of discovery. The educator becomes a kind of choreographer of discovery rather than a dispenser of information or revealed knowledge. Expertise consists not in having proven answers to the myriad questions that arise in education but in having a firm sense of possible guidelines for discovery. The role of the educator is to organize activities through which others can make discoveries. Those moments of participating in the process of discovery are proving to be memorable and even electrifying for students and family members alike.

We seek the participation of various members of the school community in the search for ways to improve the learning of all children. As a result, we are making a number of discoveries about the connections between families and schools. We are finding that one way of choreographing discoveries is through the examination of family stories and family memories. For example, discussions with teachers about grandparents as educators encouraged understanding of the complexities of families as sources of strength for those of many different backgrounds and family structures. Such illustrations of the relationships between families and learning carried ideas beyond hollow abstractions. The stories of grandparents were not only emotionally significant to those telling them but became reference points—markers—for others as well.

Gaining Insights From Family
Stories and Family Memories

Our work offers a variety of opportunities to tell and listen to family stories, including meetings with school administrators, teachers, and parents in schools across the United States. Sometimes a session is formally structured for the telling of stories, but more often family stories emerge in the context of other discussions of family-school relationships and learning in families.

Probing Family Stories and Family Memories

In emphasizing family stories, we often draw upon the research of the Elbenwood Center for the Study of the Family as Educator at Teachers College, Columbia University.[2] In the Elbenwood Center's study of family memories, a number of probes have been developed for eliciting ideas about how families construct and reconstruct memories and convey them from one generation to another. These include probes about family homes and childhood rooms, the significance of objects as memorabilia, family storytelling, memories of television viewing, family photographs, naming practices, foods and food rituals, the transmission of biography, individual memory styles and family roles in memory keeping, conflicts and disagreements about memories, and memory expeditions (see Leichter, 1996).

One probe that we found particularly useful concerns the educational views of grandparents. A way of carrying out this probe in various discussion groups is to ask participants to introduce themselves in terms of the educational views of one of their grandparents. A similar probe could focus on parents or other members of the family, but for many, the focus on grandparents enables a slight distancing. Interestingly, even where grandparents are not known—sometimes for tragic reasons—stories about them are often handed down.

The power of this probe is illustrated by the introduction of one woman who told about the words of her grandmother that have inspired her all her life and still ring in her ears today. As she explained, these inspiring words came from a grandmother who never finished grade school:

"Girl, just go on and be the best you can. You must be the best you can. You've got to do better than I've done. I wasn't able to do much because I had no help. You can go on and be more than I am. You're smart. I can give you the little bit of help that I can. Be the best you can." These are the words of my Grandma Wilma, who I called MaMa. I can still see her when I recited something at church on the stage and she would be sitting right up there in the front row. I didn't do more than say a few words of a Bible verse, but she would be beaming, just beaming. (Personal communication)

One guideline when using these probes is never to force anyone to participate who does not do so voluntarily. This relates to questions of privacy and the need to be mindful not to intrude in family relationships or to be overly inquisitive about matters that may prove painful or embarrassing. One can never know for sure what will be emotionally volatile and hard to talk about. Despite these cautions—or perhaps because of them—eliciting family memories and stories about grandparents is a productive way to understand how families help children learn.

Family stories are evocative. They remind listeners of their own stories and often almost involuntarily trigger a chain of related recollections. This is fundamental to their power to communicate and create empathy. This sometimes occurs most strikingly through small, seemingly trivial, details and vignettes. Even a secondhand report of a story may have this power. An illustration is a story told by one woman about hiding food she did not wish to eat when she was a child. At a family gathering, she stole into the backyard with the shrimp she was meant to have eaten. She had it carefully wrapped in a napkin and buried it, napkin and all. Unfortunately, she was discovered. Others often respond to the report of this story with recollections of their own about events and places where they hid undesired food as children, for example, under tables, on shelves, in the cushions of leather chairs, and in shoes. One might interpret such behavior in terms of an analysis of food and feeding practices, but the power of memory triggering is that it creates an almost involuntary set of associations. And the similarities of one experience to another, often under very different social circumstances, serve as a cautionary note against premature overinterpretation. In group discussions of the educational views of grandparents, for example, it is common for someone to report a story about a grandparent with vivid detail and intense, sometimes unexpected, emotion to which others respond with the reaction, "That reminds me of a story about my own grandparent."

Telling stories about the educational views of grandparents in discussions with teachers and school administrators also made clear, partly by indirection, that their own stories were in many respects similar to those that could be obtained from families in their schools, if appropriate vehicles for listening could be found. This is not to suggest that telling stories about grandparents is necessarily the only way to achieve empathy between families and school personnel. But it is one mode of creative experimentation.

Emerging Insights From Family
Stories and Family Memories

One insight that emerged from storytelling concerns the variety of family forms that exist today. This issue receives so much attention that it seems trivialized by repetition and general statements about respecting diversity. But stories about particular families and persons with whom individuals have shared households, lived near, or called on for assistance make exceedingly clear that a wide range of kin may be significant sources of support. An older sibling, a stepparent, an aunt or uncle, and many other kin in addition to grandparents all come up in family stories. Family stories also make it abundantly evident that changes occur over the life cycle, and family forms, such as single-parent status, may be temporary. The support of kin is clear in a story one woman told about family outings in the rural South, explaining that her grandfather built a large trailer to pull behind his car, and each year he would take all his grandchildren and as many neighborhood children as he could fit into the trailer to a local park for a big cookout. She went on to note that although the expedition gave the appearance of being her grandfather's trip, her aunts, uncles, mother, and grandmother actually did all the work. She described an old, black, cast-iron pot in which food was cooked and noted that lasting friendships developed from these picnics. This woman also reported a story about the importance of church homecomings and how proud she felt when she was allowed to sit beside her grandmother in the choir. Sometimes, such stories of kin gatherings are told with a sense of nostalgia and a concern that these extended family ties may not be as strong in the future, but such interpretations also make clear that images of family strengths and pleasures may be significant even when they do not immediately appear to be central to a family's present-day life. A related story points to the generosity that may be part of family life, even in considerable poverty. One man reported that although his family was very poor and only had two rooms for the entire family, his mother always prepared a table piled high—overflowing—with food whenever the minister would come to sit at their table.

In reflecting further on the variety of family forms, it became clear that arbitrary distinctions of social class, levels of education, wealth, and achievement were not necessarily related to educational goals and ideals. In fact, an extended family often includes persons of varied social positions. Some stories have an almost classic theme of grandparents with little formal education, perhaps immigrants, having the absolute determination to correct and compensate for their own lack of schooling by supporting the education of their children and grandchildren. An illustration is the story of one man who regularly took his children to libraries and cultural centers with the view that education and strong family ties would be his children's salvation. In an interpretive aside, he explained that this was a way of making up for his own childhood experience of being orphaned and not provided with any real direction. Stories of geographic moves from rural areas to cities and from one country to another were sometimes characterized as a way of seeking a better life for children and grandchildren and getting them out of poverty. In stories of immigration, the assistance of kin in such matters as finding loopholes in immigration quotas or offering legal sponsorship and assistance on arrival in the new country may have a ring of classic American sagas, but the details of such stories highlight the need to be mindful of the changing circumstances of families. The same is true of stories of families during particular historic events such as war and depression.

Another insight from family memories concerns the blurring of the divide between formal and informal education and the significance of self-education. Stories about grandparents, for example, sometimes describe the educational efforts and desires of those with little or no formal schooling and the extensive self-education that can take place outside of schools, from reading, traveling, and experience in work settings. When education is looked at biographically through family stories, it becomes clear that a variety of educative styles exist—ways of moving through and combining educational experiences from different sources over the life's course (Hamid, 1979;

Lagemann, 1979; Leichter, 1973). The efforts of grandparents to learn the language and culture of the United States from younger family members and more formal sources illustrate such combining. And as children teach their parents and grandparents, they may also learn through stories about their culture of origin—sometimes at unexpected moments. For example, one woman reported that her mother had long, slender, beautiful hands and nails. Compliments on her hands would trigger her mother to tell stories about the members of her childhood family in the country from which she had immigrated, all of whom had similar hands.

Another insight gained is the importance of the small details of everyday living as sources of education and the lessons—often implicit, embedded, and tacit rather than explicit and didactic—that are conveyed through everyday activities such as gardening, fishing, observing nature, and sitting on the porch and listening to gossip or talking about those who pass by. Stories about organizing kitchens, canning vegetables, or keeping household records can be vivid examples of how to manage life, with lessons that remain clear. Stories of everyday ingenuity in household work and play are illustrative. One man, for example, reported that his family was so poor that as a child he could not afford a ball, so he used tin cans to play ball with and made darts by finding tar and putting it on nails and then sticking chicken feathers in the tar.

Another insight that emerged concerns the forms that educational inspiration may take. Although one may assume, and rightly so, that personal attention, encouragement, and praise given to children (and adults as well) can stimulate the desire to learn and the confidence that it is possible to achieve, it becomes evident through family stories that many additional forms of educational encouragement—some indirect—are significant to individuals. Stories of overcoming hardship, stories of those with limited education working for the improved educational chances of their children, stories of the sacrifices that siblings make to help each other obtain education, and the household symbols—rituals, mottoes, and icons—that set forth the importance of hard work and achievement all offer vivid images of educational inspiration. One man reported with considerable emotion how important his grandfather's barn was to him because his grandfather had a sign in the barn with a motto about the value of hard work and education. Illustrations of persons unconventional and determined enough to defy traditions of their generation are reported as compelling lessons of the need to follow one's own direction. An example is the story of a great-grandmother who traveled around the world at a time when this was unheard of in her social circle.

A further insight from family stories and family memories concerns the common themes of experience among those of different backgrounds. Here, the power of stories to spark recollections of related stories comes in. A story about the smells of bread baking in the kitchen of a Norwegian grandmother in Minnesota, for example, reminded one listener of her grandmother's cooking of chicken and biscuits in a small town in Pennsylvania. The smells were different, but the vivid images triggered a rush of recollections for others. In this connection, it is significant that family stories sometimes include unexpected success in families that appear to be totally overwhelmed by problems. What is more, they cover a range of emotions, take ironic and humorous forms, and have the potential to surprise.

Occasions for Telling and Listening to Family Stories and Family Memories

There are many occasions, both formal and informal, when storytelling and listening can be used to obtain a richer, more complex understanding of the actual and potential contributions of families to their children's education. Sessions specifically structured for telling family stories and discussing memories can be extremely useful. But formal storytelling sessions are not the only way in which a deeper understanding of families can be obtained. We find a variety of other opportunities to listen for family stories in less formal settings—for example, in working to set up parent rooms in schools and doing the various housekeeping chores associated with family-school events. Stories are frequently told while other work is being carried out, even such mundane tasks as washing dishes. Indeed, such naturally occurring storytelling may have an informality, liveliness, and humor difficult to achieve in more formally structured sessions.

Although we emphatically recommend attending to stories and memories as a way of opening up one's view to a fuller picture of families, the most fundamental significance of stories may lie in their power to create a shift in ways of seeing and listening to families, especially other people's families. This may lead to the realization that other people's families are as intricate and complex as one's own. We are finding that one good step for teachers and school administrators seeking to achieve such a change in mind-set is to reflect on their own family stories and family memories.

Conserving and Conveying Discovered Insights

We think the insights achieved from attending to family stories and family memories are significant, but it is crucial to approach educational improvement through choreographing further discovery on the basis of these insights rather than treating them as solidified, fixed canons to be handed down. As Margaret Mead (1979) once asked in discussing the conservation of insight with respect to bilingual education, "Can insight be conserved or must each generation remake the same discoveries in order to have the sense of authentic participation?" (p. 144). How can one convey the wisdom and experience of one group while at the same time enabling others to make fresh discoveries without merely reinventing the wheel?

These questions are especially problematic in education where there is a tendency for "pendulum swings" and "the contribution and point of view of each age grade is bound to be infused with a certain amount of rejection of their own education as well as the usual rebellion against the senior generation" (Mead, 1979, p. 144). A helpful image, Mead suggests, is that of a spiral, or the return to similar issues, but at a new level, based on the experience of others.

Because approaches to guiding spontaneous discovery have not been widely developed in recent educational scholarship, particularly research seeking empirical proof of connections between variables and reports of tested findings, we believe the spiral image is useful. This is particularly true because even where a project has empirical findings to report, in applying these findings to further practice, it is still necessary to choreograph discoveries about applications (Leichter & Mitchell, 1978). To be sure, there are historic precedents for thinking about educational discovery. Yet, when funders and supporters of social programs want proof that their resources are being well used, achieving narrowly conceived measures of success sometimes becomes an end in itself, replacing careful consideration of applications and next steps as well as the fundamental purposes of education. These issues of how to convey insights from school improvement efforts are of general significance. But they have particular force in considering families and education because so many emotionally charged beliefs and simplified answers, so much musing and moralizing (Leichter, 1974), come up when families—especially other people's families—are the concern.

The idea of partnership between home and school illustrates this point. Although much good work goes on in education today using the rubric of partnership as a guide to parent involvement and cooperation between families and schools, the idea is sometimes phrased in such general terms that it has the aura of a truism—it cannot be faulted—and yet it lacks the adequate imagery for working out particular situations that may arise under different circumstances with different families. Home visits are an example. It is easy to recommend enabling teachers to gain a better understanding of the environments from which children come, and teachers visiting homes is one such vehicle. Yet, circumstances can easily be imagined in which not all reactions to home visits are positive. It is useful to consider the prospect of a teacher coming to visit one's own home and noting that however well-intentioned the purpose of learning more about the family may be, the anticipated visit does not necessarily seem different from a visit by a professional such as a welfare worker coming to inspect and judge and perhaps recommend the removal of one's financial supports. Therefore, in reporting that some schools find home visits to be effective and valued by both teachers and families, it is necessary to describe these successes in ways that do not gloss over the complexities and possible counterreactions. Otherwise, the report will lack authenticity and risk becoming sentimental and platitudinous at best or simplistic and condescending at worst. At the very least, an effort is required to view any set of proposed actions—especially remedial actions—from the perspective of the various participants involved. Attending to family stories and family memories, as we have shown, is one way of looking at issues from multiple perspectives. Still, an issue remains of how to find general principles while at the same time allowing for the complexity and idiosyncrasies of the particular.

Issues for Further Discovery

Following the spiral image, one approach to conserving and conveying the insights from our work thus far is to consider at a somewhat more abstract level those issues that inhere in the insights we obtained from attending to family stories. The purpose here is to gain even greater understanding of how families and schools may join together to help children receive a high-quality education.

Communication Between Families and Schools Across Backgrounds

A general issue in thinking about collaboration between families and schools concerns the conditions under which those of different backgrounds can communicate most effectively with each other. Communication with families about their children's schooling is always delicate and emotionally charged, and privacy and confidentiality are significant concerns. Although all families have problems, some are more open in discussion of them. Here, perceived status relations between school personnel and family members may come into play. If, for example, a teacher is seen as more educated than members of a family, this higher status—or perceived higher status— may be a reason for reluctance in conveying that which is deemed shameful and inelegant. By contrast, if a teacher is deemed to be less successful—less well paid—than members of the family, this may be a reason for doubting the teacher's competence to make judgments about the family. In either case, perceived status is crucial.

The classic discussion by the sociologist Robert K. Merton (1972- 1973) about insiders and outsiders is pertinent to thinking about who can work with whom. Much rhetoric and facile discussion is to be found on this topic, with some arguing that effective communication can only take place between those of similar backgrounds. Indeed, there are good reasons to presume that communication is different when common reference and common framing of questions is possible. Under such circumstances, many facets of a communication can be taken for granted and do not require explicit spelling out. In analyzing how stories are told, it has been shown, for example, using an illustration of tape-recorded material from a storyteller before and after he became a professional storyteller, that the framing and format of the story when told among local friends at a fishing camp was quite distinct from the framing of the same core story when it was told to a large audience, unfamiliar with the local setting, at a professional folklore conference. In the latter case, a good deal of explanation about the nature of the setting, the location, and the character of the local environment was added to make the story comprehensible to outsiders (Bauman, 1986).

As Merton (1972-1973) points out, however, the concept of insider and outsider needs to be qualified by considering the multiple statuses or roles that all individuals in society hold. For example, a young, Irish American woman from the South is different from an older, Italian American woman from the South. Yet, the two women, who differ in age and ethnic background, nonetheless have in common the fact that they are both women and come from the South. In ethnic background and age, they are outsiders to each other, but in gender and place, they are insiders.

The idea of multiple statuses is of considerable significance in thinking about strategies of communication and who can work with whom under what circumstances as it suggests that there are often common insider relationships on which to build even when major differences of background also exist. Therefore, if a vehicle for learning from families can be found, those in schools attempting to work more closely with families in some respects different in background from their own may have more options in finding common points of reference than initially appears.

Variations in Family Structure and Household Composition

The forms that families take in contemporary society are much discussed at present. Certain family forms, such as single-parent families, receive particular attention and are often treated as if uniformity existed within the category—as if all single-parent families were alike—and as if they were by definition deviant and problematic, a reflection of a deteriorating society. In such formulations, the fact that single-parent families existed in earlier times (for example, as a result of the death of a spouse) is overlooked. Such categorical images make it difficult to see the strengths in families with a composition not in keeping with some idealized, imagined norm. Given the great variety of families from which schoolchildren come and the variety of caretakers that represent them (for example, parents, grandparents, siblings, uncles, and aunts) it is important to find ways to understand these families in their own terms.

The difficulty of understanding the great variety of families is further complicated by the fact that all families change considerably over their life cycle, with the addition of new members, the growth of children, and the departure of members. Indeed, as parents often wistfully note when their children are about to leave home, the strenuous and sometimes overpowering responsibilities they felt when their children were young seem in retrospect to have lasted only too brief a time. And the much discussed phases of child development appear to occur with such lightning speed that adjustments to one phase, such as the terrible twos, are barely made when adjustments to another phase, such as the teenage years, are required. Single-parent families, too, change over their life course, and single-parent status may in fact be a momentary arrangement. In addition, numerous instabilities are associated with a rapidly changing society, such as geographic moves, loss of employment, lack of housing, and lack of health coverage. At one level, these issues are so familiar as to be obvious, but it requires a sustained effort to understand how they play out in particular ways for various families—a sustained effort to learn from families.

The Educational Roles of Families, Schools, and Communities

Another general issue to which we believe it is useful to return with further efforts to choreograph discoveries is defining the parameters of the educational roles of those in schools, families, and community institutions. If one looks historically at relationships between families and schools, for example, following the work of Lawrence Cremin (1990), it is clear that there are changes under different social conditions in what are considered to be the essential responsibilities of families in relation to those of schools. Schools as we know them today are comparatively new and very different in their responsibilities from what they have been at other times. Larry Cuban's (1992) analysis of schools as legatee institutions or legatee functions is also significant. As the form and function of families and the place that they have in the economy changes—for example, as more women enter the workforce outside the home and families are less often a unit of production than they sometimes were in agricultural settings—schools are seen to take on new roles that previously were seen to belong to families.

In attempts to define the educational roles of families, schools, and community institutions, the deeply emotional character of family relationships is significant. Clearly, family ties can be sources of both joy and emotional distress, and it is evident that emotional distress of numerous kinds can have an impact on children's learning. One cannot presume that mere information about child-rearing practices will be sufficient to counteract the conflicts and other sources of distress that influence children's learning. The divide between educational and quasi-therapeutic roles is seldom clear-cut. It is one thing, for example, to discuss with a parent the behavioral problems of a child in school and how these might be corrected through reorganization of the space in the home, changes in the family's management of time, or more emphasis on homework. It is quite another matter to talk about how and whether the child's problems are a reflection of difficulties in the marriage or the separation or single-parent status of one of the parents. Yet, given one of the canons of family therapy, that the problems of one member, particularly a child, may reflect problems of others, it is important to think about families from multiple perspectives.

In seeking to define the roles of families, schools, and community institutions, it is important for professionals to resist the temptation to tell families how they should solve their problems or bring up their children. In this connection, it may be useful for school administrators and teachers to be prepared with referrals for assistance that goes beyond the limits that school personnel can legitimately and comfortably offer. In some schools with which we have worked, for example, school administrators have found that keeping maps and charts of the community's social services is useful. What is more, the distinction between professional knowledge and everyday knowledge is seldom as sharply defined as is sometimes imagined. Teachers and school administrators are also themselves family members, and many of their professional ideas about the family are overlaid with their own personal experiences. In the same way, family members who are not professional educators may also have access to ideas about the family from other professionals. In fact, the popularization of many kinds of psychological thinking about families and the extent that this is covered in the media—in soap operas, talk shows, news editorials, and news coverage—means that ideas about the family are readily available. What is sometimes called the blurring of genres or distinctions between everyday and professional knowledge is considerable. If this blurring is recognized, it means that an understanding of the family's ideas about the functioning of the family is a source on which professionals may draw. It also means that the professional expertise is less mysterious, less distinct, and in a sense, less authoritative than might otherwise be the case. In this connection, a respectful approach to families is one in which an effort is made to work collaboratively so that, as Melva D. Burke (1994) puts it, the need to know meets the need to tell. It also means that sustained efforts to find new ways to learn from families, particularly how family members see and interpret the world, are important.

The Sources of Education in Families and Communities

Another issue for which we believe it is useful to choreograph further discoveries concerns the nature and quality of the many forms of education in families and communities. Mapping and examining the education that goes forward in the various educational institutions in society—those that constitute the configurations of educational institutions—is one important step (Cremin, 1979). The need to examine the role of the media in the education that takes place in the home is an illustration. At present, the media significantly alter the information that comes into the home and the kinds of education that take place there. This means that creative reexamination of the roles of families and schools is important, particularly as new technologies are increasingly brought into schools and the technology available in the home changes.

Another fundamental and complex issue is that of how the culture of the home and the culture of the school are related. An examination of these issues needs to be carefully made with consideration of the perspectives of the various participants. As the history of schooling for Native Americans in the United States attests, there have been times when schools took on the function of acculturation in ways that were heavy-handed and colonialist, with the assumption that Native American students should be removed from their homes, taken to boarding schools, and educated in new ways for their own good. In such instances, the school was seen to have the responsibility not merely of a legatee institution that filled in the points where the family was unable to educate but also one with the responsibility of substituting a culture different from that of the home. The reports of Erik Erikson (1950) and others (e.g., Bordewich, 1996) concerning the schooling of Native American children sound extreme, yet a complex dilemma exists regarding how to educate in standard modes that enable the support and development of a national culture while at the same time respecting local identities and the multiple local cultures that are to be found in schools throughout the United States today. What is more, the importance of these issues is augmented as the transnational migration of populations increases and new views of the significance of cultural identity come under discussion. In short, issues of the cultures of the home and the cultures of the school and how these may be brought together in creative amalgams respectful of the various points of view are of central importance in work with schools today. We believe that a respectful examination of these topics can be orchestrated through further efforts to learn from families so that it becomes possible to achieve an appreciation of the cultures of the home that goes beyond abstractions and platitudes about multiculturalism.

Continuing Reflections

In seeking ways to improve cooperation among families, schools, and communities and to enhance the contributions of families to their children's education, we need to find new lenses for viewing families, new ways of learning from families. Attending to family stories and family memories is one way to get beyond simplified conceptions, or what Gregory Bateson (1972) calls "dormitive concepts"—concepts that explain away and put thinking to sleep. Stories help to set the stage for creative discussions. Stories are also important because they offer opportunities for families to make ideas their own. The transmission of ideas from one generation to another is not a simple, linear process of handing down unchanged ways of life but rather a question of how each generation can offer the next generation raw materials with which to create its own sagas and identities. It is especially important to discover ways in which these raw materials can be made vital rather than inert. This also applies to the ideas that are transmitted among families, schools, and other institutions. In attempting to choreograph further discoveries, we believe it is possible through the use of stories to create a spiral whereby each return to general issues adds fresh insights to previous considerations.

Yet, stories are seldom finished and complete. One should not expect all insights from stories to be acted on immediately. Some may remain latent as a pool of images and ideas on which to draw as new occasions arise. Stories offer new ways of carrying forward a continuing search for connections between families, schools, and communities. And because children, too, learn from stories, stories offer valuable opportunities for discovering ways to support the learning of all children. For the moment, the hope is that those educators thinking about the possibilities inherent in family stories and family memories will reflect on their own and respond to those of others with, "That reminds me of a story!"

Notes

I wish to express my appreciation to Susan Heath for insightful comments and valuable suggestions on the manuscript. I also wish to thank the members of the National Coalition who met in New Mexico in summer 1996 to discuss this volume. Their ideas were helpful in the formulation of this chapter.

1. For present purposes, I use the terms *family stories* and *family memories* interchangeably. Distinctions may, of course, be drawn between stories and memories, but because the terms are evocative in different ways, it seems appropriate to use both in this discussion. Moreover, in the sense that memories are stories, over time they have special significance for understanding families.

2. Support for these studies came from a Guggenheim Fellowship to Hope Jensen Leichter for a study of the role of memory in the family; from the Spencer Foundation for general support of the Elbenwood Center, a study of social networks and educative styles, and a study of the mediation of television by the family; and from the Ford Foundation for a study of grandparents as educators of young children. The work of the Elbenwood Center was also made possible by the generous endowment of Ben and Grace Wood.

References

American education: Still separate, still unequal. (1995, Fall). *Daedalus: Journal of the American Academy of Arts and Sciences* [Special issue].

Bateson, G. (1972). *Steps to an ecology of mind.* New York: Ballantine.

Bateson, G. (1979). *Mind and nature: A necessary unity.* New York: Dutton.

Bauman, R. (1986). *Story, performance and event: Contextual studies of oral narrative.* Cambridge, UK: Cambridge University Press.

Bordewich, E. M. (1996). *Killing the white man's Indian: Reinventing Native Americans at the end of the 20th century.* New York: Doubleday.

Bruner, J. (1990). *Acts of meaning.* Cambridge, MA: Harvard University Press.

Burke, M. D. (1994). *Black grandparenting: The ties that bind.* Unpublished Ed.D. dissertation, Teachers College, Columbia University.

Cremin, L. A. (1979). Family-community linkages in American education: Some comments on the recent historiography. In H. J. Leichter (Ed.), *Families and communities as educators* (pp. 119-140). New York: Teachers College Press.

Cremin, L. A. (1990). *Popular education and its discontents.* New York: Harper & Row.

Cuban, L. (1992, February). Why some reforms last: The case of the kindergarten. *American Journal of Education, 166,* 166-194.

Dyson, A. H., & Genishi, C. (Eds.). (1994). *The need for story: Cultural diversity in classroom and community.* Urbana, IL: National Council of Teachers of English.

Erikson, E. (1950). *Childhood and society.* New York: Norton.

Graham, P. A. (1995, Fall). Battleships and schools. In American education: Still separate, still unequal [Special issue]. *Daedalus: Journal of the American Academy of Arts and Sciences,* 43-46.

Hamid, V. (1979). *Social class variations in educative styles: Two case studies.* Unpublished Ed.D. dissertation, Teachers College, Columbia University.

Howe, H., II. (1995, Fall). Priority strategies for improved learning. In American education: Still separate, still unequal [Special issue]. *Daedalus: Journal of the American Academy of Arts and Sciences,* 69-76.

Kozol, J. (1991). *Savage inequalities: Children in America's schools.* New York: Harper Perennial.

Lagemann, E. C. (1979). *A generation of women: Education in the lives of progressive reformers.* Cambridge, MA: Harvard University Press.

Leichter, H. J. (1973). The concept of educative style. *Teachers College Record, 76,* 175-217.

Leichter, H. J. (1974). *The family as educator.* New York: Teachers College Press.

Leichter, H. J. (Ed.). (1979). *Families and communities as educators.* New York: Teachers College Press.

Leichter, H. J. (1996). Creative intelligence of families: Bridges to school learning. *Equity and Excellence in Education: The University of Massachusetts School of Education Journal, 29*(1), 77-85.

Leichter, H. J., & Mitchell, W. E. (1978). *Kinship and casework: Family networks and social intervention* (Rev. ed.). New York: Teachers College Press.

Mead, M. (1979). The conservation of insight: Educational under-standing of bilingualism. In H. J. Leichter (Ed.), *Families and communities as educators* (pp. 141-157). New York: Teachers College Press.

Merton, R. K. (1972-1973). Insiders and outsiders: A chapter in the sociology of knowledge. *American Journal of Sociology, 78,* 9-47.

Paley, V. G. (1981). *Wally's stories.* Cambridge, MA: Harvard University Press.

6 Toward Equality Schools

VALERIE WHEELER

WARD J. GHORY

ROBERT L. SINCLAIR

Public schools are responsible for ensuring that all citizens, not just an elite few, are prepared for success in our society. Significant progress is being made to accomplish this end, but much work remains to be done. For example, the greatest division in our country is between those who develop the academic competencies and social skills needed to realize the American dream and those who do not have a fair chance for economic security, meaningful work, and constructive civic involvement. This is why we consider equality in public schools a primary focus for reform. Educators need to create conditions so that all children learn well, regardless of the inequality of their circumstances. Our work in schools and school systems across the country shows that some schools are more effective than others in helping children succeed in their learning and preparing them for constructive participation in society. In this chapter, we introduce the idea of an "Equality School" as a way to explore characteristics that emerge in schools where all students are helped to realize their academic and personal promise.

This chapter has three major, interrelated parts. First, we bring forward for consideration educators' images of greater equality in local schools. These images guide thinking and action in Equality Schools. Second, we describe the common characteristics of Equality Schools so that we can explore the special nature of learning environments where the goal of equality is taken seriously. Finally, we reflect on the cooperation among educators that is necessary for local schools to make equality a reality for learning.

Images of Schools That Promote Equality

In the early 19th century, Horace Mann's "common schools" recalled Thomas Jefferson's fundamental belief that a democratic government depended on an educated citizenry. Jefferson stated, "I know no safe depository of the ultimate powers of the society but the people themselves, and if we think them not enlightened enough to exercise their control in a wholesome discretion, the remedy is not to take it from them, but to inform their discretion by education" (quoted in Soder, 1996, p. 129). Although the overall quality of schooling that eventually emerged from the common school is a matter for debate, the intention to create good schools for all young people was implicit. Horace Mann was a visionary who saw the potential of education as a gateway to equality.

From the "efficient schools" of the 1920s (Callahan, 1962) to John Goodlad's (1963) "nongraded school" in the 1960s, efforts to realign public schools and democracy include attempts to maintain an implicit image of a good school, a school where opportunities for success in learning are fairly and impartially opened to all students, including those who are marginal in their learning. More recent efforts, such as Mortimer Adler's (1982) "Paideia school," Henry Levin's (1987) "accelerated school," and Theodore Sizer's (1992) "essential school," explicitly outline imperatives the reformers consider necessary for creating school environments that better foster the learning of all students. As educators face decisions in their classrooms and schools, they are guided by often unexplored images of how a school works best to provide high-quality schooling for all on equal terms. By bringing such images into sharp focus around the idea of an Equality School, we begin to clarify the vision of educators looking for ways to help every student learn well so that he or she may become a productive citizen.

To this end, we join with educators in local schools to create conditions that are responsive to the varied needs of diverse individuals and sensitive to the persistent demands of the democratic society in which they live. As a result of their commitment to the belief that it is possible for educators to design conditions in schools and classrooms so that all students reach high levels of academic accomplishment, 20 individual schools around the country entered into an experiment to become "Equality Schools."[1] As pioneers in the ongoing drive to plan and implement schools appropriate in a democracy, these schools are making significant progress in providing a high-quality education for all children, even those youngsters who are living and trying to learn in adverse circumstances.

In the most simple terms, an Equality School is a good school, one where all students of all families are learning well. It is a place where the spirit as well as the mind are nurtured and challenged. Here, learning by conditioning is replaced by learning through the practice of creative intelligence. Forward-looking educators in these schools construct learning environments where children from different backgrounds live and learn together in ways that help all youngsters succeed in school. Their success is determined by how well everyone learns, not by the accomplishments of a few. Equality Schools, then, are places where each student finds and develops something of value on which to build a life while learning to appreciate what others offer as well. In an Equality School, the right to an education and the resources available to advance high-quality learning are balanced in such a way that all students receive their optimal benefit. To create equality in school is to promote democracy in society. In Equality Schools, this is the image that encourages careful decisions and fosters bold actions.

Unfortunately, too many schools in our communities today are places where necessary resources are disproportionately allocated. Educators' main concerns are usually for the highly achieving students, viewed as "the best" in the school. These top students seem to get the best teachers, the best schedules, the most attention. Sometimes, a school within a school is created to provide a special setting for these star students. The glittering accomplishments of these elite learners are the pride of the community, the hallmark for what makes the school good. Yet, in and around these schools, nagging questions remain. How equitable is the access to the best learning environments?[2] What is the plight of the learner with average scores in the high-achieving environment? Who goes lacking while others gain? When we hear of a good school, it seems that there is no assurance that equality is an imperative for learning or that diversity is a strength of community. Too often in these schools, youngsters are sorted into top, middle, and bottom groups where they are expected to learn at different rates and various levels of accomplishment. The result is that many children are forced to the margins of school life where they do not benefit in fair and proportional ways from the environment intended to help all of them succeed in their learning.

Educators in Equality Schools, however, take action for learning by asking, "Under what particular conditions do individual students learn well?" In Equality Schools, educators look first to the student, realizing that individuals learn—groups do not learn. These schools include varied conditions forming a unique learning community in which diversity is recognized and supported instead of ignored and suppressed. Nothing short of an enduring commitment to all our children learning from challenging educational experiences will suffice if we truly expect public schools to progress anywhere close to a state of both excellence and equality. This is another image that guides educators who lead Equality Schools.

Characteristics of Equality Schools

Given the variability of learners and the diversity of school environments, there is no universal formula defining conditions under which all students learn well. Yet, intriguing possibilities emerge when educators and parents start to identify and resolve important problems blocking the learning of students in particular schools. We begin to see characteristics that may be common to Equality Schools. The intention is not to suggest that all of these characteristics exist in each location, all of the time, and at the same intensity. Rather, the purpose is to explore the possibilities of equality that can be realized by determined educators in local schools. Collectively, seven characteristics can be seen to form the personality, or ecology, of schools in which educators are trying to reach all students. These characteristics give texture to the educational environments in Equality Schools. Let us consider briefly each of these characteristics in turn.

In Equality Schools, educators believe that all children have the capacity to learn at high levels of accomplishment and a right to a high-quality education on equal terms. Equality Schools operate on the premise that all students are capable of high levels of intellectual accomplishment, including those young people who are failing or underachieving. Educators in these schools are discovering that students differ more in the speed and mode in which they learn than in what they are capable of learning. These discoveries naturally have far-reaching implications for how instruction is organized and delivered. Furthermore, teachers and principals are finding that factors frequently examined as potential barriers to learning—such as race, ethnicity, gender, socioeconomic status, or household composition—do not necessarily impede child development or learning. The crucial issue here is that educators in Equality Schools recognize their responsibility to adapt their practices to solve learning problems, regardless of the students' starting point or the circumstances surrounding their lives. Learning is the result of interaction between the child and the environment. Hence, failure is not attributable to what is in the child alone.

All teachers do not walk through the school doors with these beliefs. Such matters of conviction have to be established explicitly in faculty meetings and study teams that gather after students have left for the day. A good part of the work in an Equality School is to develop a platform of premises to guide thoughts and actions. Educators in local schools are challenged to define the major problems their own students are having with their learning. Discussion of these problems may strike deeply at the pride and the self-doubts of teachers and principals, making discussion sometimes sharply realistic about what common learning can be expected from all children. It takes time, trouble, and leadership from several quarters to develop a consensus to support and sustain school improvement and foster increased learning. An important characteristic of Equality Schools, then, is an explicit commitment to spirited dialogue and mindful action, guided by articulated premises about the importance of reaching all students. It seems reasonable for educators striving to make their schools Equality Schools to craft a statement of beliefs that is written at the local school and agreed to by all faculty. We find that agreement on such premises is a prerequisite for searching and constructive self-study and meaningful and lasting reform.

In Equality Schools, educators can identify the real problems block-ing the learning of students and set priorities for improving the learning of all students so that problem solving becomes a way of life. So much energy in schools goes into carrying the established program forward in tried-and-true ways that it is a real accomplishment for school staffs to step back from their demanding routine and agree on the most troubling problems that face their students. Some of the problems teachers and principals find in this process are their own problems as individuals and groups, so identifying them requires an unusual level of honesty and group self-awareness. When mature faculty members define learning problems and con-sider the obstacles in the school and home environments that may be blocking learning, they can better set priorities for improved learning. Study teams are often formed to carry on the analysis and devise and try out solutions. This keeps the focus on the ends the participants are trying to accomplish and helps them avoid being seduced by the facile adoption of the first suggested means that come to mind for intervention. In Equality Schools, we find that a momentum is created for improvement by careful adherence to a simple planning cycle: problem identification, priority setting, experimentation with interventions, reflections on results, and reconsideration of the problem.

Staff at one of the early schools recognized as an Equality School, the Mildred Jenkins Elementary School in Spring, Texas, set a priority to improve reading comprehension for every student. Three study teams went into action: weekly child study teams focused on stu-dents at risk of failure due to severe reading difficulties; a broader study team looked at special groups of students and reasons for trouble in reading comprehension, offering an opportunity for pro-fessional development for the staff as well as a forum for planning reading instruction; a third body, a campus advisory committee, including parents, teachers, and administrators, met monthly to pay attention to the so-called average student who might be overlooked. This group also mobilized community support for students in need of medical, housing, food, or other social services. The combined efforts of the study teams created a series of improvements, including 14 changes in the roles and responsibilities of faculty to provide a more balanced instructional staff at each grade level, redirection of existing funds for reading improvement, before- and after-school tutorials for marginal students, recognition programs for readers, and school-business partnerships providing incentives for reading gains. Not only did children's reading scores rise on annual state achievement tests, but all members of the school community felt a sense of energy, enthusiasm, and excitement emerge from their positive forward momentum. It seems that once this cycle begins in an Equality School, problem solving becomes a way of life.

In Equality Schools, it is possible to help all students learn well without holding back any children who have a history of excellence in learning. In most schools where resources are tightly stretched, the prospect of reaching out to even more students to help them learn well creates the fear that other children will now backslide or suffer. The fear is that resources will be redirected away from those who have been succeeding and given to others in need and that this will be done at the expense of those who excelled in the past. What we find in Equality Schools is that everyone gains when learning activities promote participation for all students.

At the Winship Elementary School in Spring, Texas, the faculty agreed on a profoundly simple priority—to challenge every child every day. Faculty members wanted to motivate and catch up students who were falling behind while keeping their "achieving majority" moving quickly through its paces. This simple principle—every child, every day—meant that no one should go home without learning something new. The idea had unassailable appeal, and it sharpened teachers' and students' critical awareness about who was making important progress. The pursuit of activities that challenge the student at the top of the class and also encourage the student previously at the bottom of the class is an ongoing one that spawned notable increases in parental involvement and the reorganization of special education resources so that sorting is replaced by inclusion.

Equality Schools, virtually by definition, are concerned that progress for some is not at the expense of others. This concern leads to productive exchanges among teachers searching for better ways to create and organize physical, social, and intellectual conditions in classrooms so that the entire range of students stays involved and productive. Also, in Equality Schools, teachers continually experiment with clever ways to keep tabs on the progress of individuals. In this sense, the mission of Equality Schools directs educators to professional development concerns, and a lively, critical curiosity about student learning results from the desire to help all children reach high levels of accomplishment.

In Equality Schools, children are not sorted into permanent group-ings that suggest that some children are better than others. One stub-born obstacle to equality in school settings is the belief by many educators that students need to be sorted to be taught efficiently. Most evaluation systems used in schools reinforce this presump-tion by rewarding those at high levels of achievement with steady promotion to exclusive learning environments with increasingly more abundant resources to promote advanced learning. These high-status settings bring together top teachers, rigorous curricu-lum, and dynamic students in a potent mix. Outside these special places, however, learning often languishes among those who start to believe that they do not have all that it takes and that they cannot be all that they would like to be. Even farther out on the fringes are the dumping grounds, such as special education or alternative schools in some districts, where students who do not fit into the prevailing learning environment are consigned and accommodated without real prospects.

In Equality Schools, educators recognize that all learners are not created equal in their discrete abilities. But these educators believe that by looking broadly at the range of human talents and skills it is possible to find in every unique child human strengths that deserve to be celebrated and developed. The more narrow the range of talents that are celebrated in school, the more likely it is that groups need to be formed to separate those most accomplished in the selected talent from those less skilled. Because a wide range of children's abilities and preparation presents a management challenge for a teacher, tempo-rary groupings can make sense for specific purposes. These may be teachable groups that dissolve after their purpose is accomplished. In Equality Schools, the emphasis is on finding ways to capitalize on human diversity. Educators look for ways to enrich instruction through the inclusion of a variety of students. They make sure that groupings remain flexible, so that all students meet on common ground for most of the day. For this reason, we have seen a significant decline in the number of students identified for special education and a change in the design of special education services in Equality Schools. The members of the special education staff now work in coteaching arrangements in the regular classrooms. In Equality

Schools, educators recognize and treat human variability in different ways, but they are committed to allocating their resources so that the total group benefits from these differences without allowing the advantages to accrue only to a favored few.

In Equality Schools, diversity is recognized as a strength for promoting learning. Many schools we serve across the country have seen the level of racial, economic, linguistic, and cultural diversity increase steadily among their students. Demographically, the face of the United States is once again changing, bringing with these changes new realities and exciting possibilities for public schools. When students from many backgrounds sit around the same table, their voices can reveal unexpected facets to familiar material and their questions can raise surprising lines of inquiry. In Equality Schools, we are finding that it is possible to create a curriculum that is sensitive to the contributions of children from differing ethnic groups and various circumstances while also emphasizing the commonalities that unite all individual students. This is being done by teachers interested in expanding their repertoire of materials and committed to finding books and situations for study where all of their children can see their own reflections illuminated in the curriculum. As the canon of stimulating works evolves to include voices from previously unstudied cultures, perennial questions are raised in fresh ways that benefit children from every group.

In Equality Schools, one of the priorities that keeps teachers strengthening their leadership and improving their learning is creating ways to draw on the diversity of their students as a compelling means to promote learning. Particularly in middle schools and high schools, the students themselves are the best advocates for the advantages of diversity and a powerful source of challenge and inspiration for teachers and other students. At Apple Valley High School in Rosemount, Minnesota, for example, the entire school community watched and listened intently as an improvisational troupe of Apple Valley students dramatized the cross-cultural clashes that had begun to occur as the school's population changed both ethnically and economically. These performances placed the school on alert and catalyzed concern. Similarly, multicultural student congresses, gay-straight clubs, student councils, and school newspaper staffs can be outstanding leaders for changes in school climate that make the environment more welcoming to diversity. In Equality Schools, we have seen that students are the best role models for other students and that their voices are the best motivators for teachers to expand the scope of their curriculum.

In Equality Schools, leadership comes from all members of the educational community as they consider conditions that facilitate or hinder learning in school. We find that people in most Equality Schools become skeptical about relying on top-down leadership as a way of promoting significant improvement. When the premium is placed on identifying and resolving problems that are blocking learning of individual students, the leadership of people closest to the learners—their parents, guardians, and teachers— naturally becomes paramount. In Equality Schools, it is clear that parents and guardians can work cooperatively with teachers to promote the learning of their children. In fact, significant progress with individuals having difficulty learning does not normally occur until the strengths of the home setting are combined with the strengths of the learning environment at school. All of the Equality Schools find it important to bring parents into the school in more meaningful roles than fund-raisers or audience members. Some Equality Schools started parent resource centers; others included parents on advisory councils; many improved parent-teacher conferences; and still others emphasized getting to know parents, grandparents, and other guardians through home visits. For example, at the Juan Linn Math and Science Magnet School in Victoria, Texas, the greatest "high-risk venture" teachers undertook as an Equality School was to visit the homes of each of their 670 students as a way of becoming familiar with the environment that supported learning at home. Because student achievement tends to increase when parents are familiar with the goals and directions of the curriculum, teachers in Equality Schools also seek to communicate with parents about their purposes, programs, and progress through newsletters, curriculum reports, student exhibitions, and evening meetings with members of the local community. Along with respecting the diversity of students goes the necessity of tapping the many strengths in the home cultures of students.

Similarly, the role of teacher as leader is expected and appreciated in Equality Schools. Although a principal may orchestrate, teachers as talented soloists or harmonized groups make the real music. In Equality Schools, most study teams are led by teachers, not administrators. Priorities are set by the faculty and administration working in concert, not announced from on high. When the emphasis is on improving learning, the varieties of teacher expertise also come into focus. In Equality Schools, teachers' involvement increases as they find avenues for real leadership development.

In Equality Schools, educators can develop an internal capacity to evaluate student progress, teacher effectiveness, and the quality of their school. When a school faculty sets priorities and tries to find solutions to learning problems, it needs to know whether learning is actually improving. Educators in Equality Schools find it is not enough to wait for the results of the next round of standardized tests, in which test items may not directly match the school's objectives, to see if they made wise choices in their interventions to help children increase their learning. Instead, teachers in Equality Schools develop the capacity to evaluate their own progress so that they can continuously use data about children's learning to increase the effectiveness of their work.

As educators in Equality Schools create ways to evaluate their own progress, they discover the need to refine and restate their priorities, moving from the general to the particular, setting more objective criteria for judging if desired outcomes are accomplished. They become more purposeful and systematic about evaluation, planning data collection at the same time they determine new problem-solving strategies. Annual evaluation reports to the community become more subtle, precise, and complete as they fight the tendency to highlight positive information and downplay or ignore negative information. With the help of national and district study teams on evaluation, such as the one in Victoria, Texas, about alternative means of assessment and the one in Spring, Texas, about evaluating learning priorities, teachers and principals in Equality Schools become more scientific and professional in their use of measurement techniques. In Equality Schools, evaluation is viewed as a helpful instrument for improvement, not a club wielded by outside powers.

Taken together, then, the seven emerging characteristics we are discovering in Equality Schools suggest new agendas for improving schools that flow from the commitment to helping all children learn well. More than any other feature, what is common to Equality Schools is the willingness of their faculty to inquire into the sources and solutions of learning problems in a manner that keeps equality foremost in mind. What teachers remember most from their struggles to make sense of complicated learning issues is the camaraderie and satisfaction that grow as they progress in their effectiveness to dialogue together. For example, as the Casey Middle School faculty in Boulder, Colorado, grappled with the implications of rapid demographic change in the student population of the school, staff members discovered that they must reach beneath the first level of understanding of diversity brought to them by guest speakers and workshops on multiculturalism. By starting a reading group of teachers and parents that evolved into a study team, they gradually began to ask and answer genuinely self-critical questions about their responsiveness to diversity and their understanding of communality. A deeper level of trust and shared purpose evolved. In short, the success of an Equality School ultimately hinges on the quality of its problem-solving dialogues.

Careful Thinking and Action in Equality Schools

The evolution of an Equality School begins with questioning by members of the school community whether all of their children are succeeding in their learning. Leaders from every cranny in the school soon realize there is no fixed solution or ready-made program that will apply to the special problems and resources in their very own dynamic and changing school culture. Once members of a local school community recognize that there are infinite routes of action, rather than assume there is only one way to improve learning, they are ready to begin a process of shared inquiry into the causes and possible solutions of learning difficulties. Also, they quickly identify and celebrate the common strengths of all students and the particular strengths of individual children.

An educator's reflections and actions arise from both intellect and intuition. There develops the continual inclination to inquire into what is needed for each student to experience success in the classroom and sense the excitement and power of learning. No one can effectively do this work for anyone else. We are seeing that a sense of inquiry must occur first on an individual level. At first, this is difficult work, but it is essential if educators are to grow in their capacity to be effective in efforts to educate young people. In turn, as teachers and principals begin to develop their own creative intelligence and reach students, they become personal and academic catalysts for others to begin crafting their ideas from understandings of the needs of children in their particular learning environment.

Equality Schools provide a setting and impetus for educators individually and collectively to develop ways to formulate and act on essential questions about effective teaching and learning. Working to change oneself can be a difficult challenge and a slow process; it requires intentionality, long-range commitment, a constant eye to one's vision, and careful thoughts about one's leadership. Gordon Anderson, Superintendent of Spring Texas Independent School District, notes that, "You cannot legislate changes in human behavior. Lasting change comes from within the hearts and minds of individuals" (personal communication, June 1996).

Too often, educators decline the ever-present invitation to lead and choose instead to reside in what are maybe more comfortable, and possibly less effective, positions of accepting answers from those who are distant from the realities persisting in schools, classrooms, and homes. Teachers and principals exist on these professional margins of inactivity and remain so primarily because they do not take the opportunity to pursue the difficult, interesting, and relevant questions about their work with students that are posed by placing value on equality. They become comfortable imitating the successes of others. It is odd how the same educators who loudly voice dissatisfaction with children's learning become so easily preoccupied with means while ignoring ends. Under such circumstances, difficult questions become boundaries rather than openings for growth and creativity.

When we speak of marginality in public schools, we are referring fundamentally to our students who exist on the margins of successful learning, but the learning community in an Equality School attends to the marginality of all individuals, educators and students alike. In essence, we seek to be at the edge of our perceptions all the time. From there, we can ask another vexing question, "What do we do about what we see and know?"

Educators who are prompted to follow the latent urge to affect change in themselves bring their views on education and their perceptions about their own setting into sharp focus. They question their relation to the prevailing conditions and act on their ideas for solving learning problems. Given responsibility for raising and answering questions, educators in local schools bring forth their most powerful creative tool, engaged and creative human intelligence. Is this not what we hope for for all learners? Any effort to improve schools or increase student learning that does not include the invocation of creative and engaged human intelligence as a functional imperative takes its first and last steps as an ineffective entity for creating equality in school.

Closing

In sum, ideas about improving schools are guided by visions of those who work and teach in them. Unless their image of a desirable school is made explicit through continuing dialogue between the faculty and parents in a local community, there is a risk that improvement efforts will lose direction and get swept away by educational fads or pressing political pressures. Attempts to create Equality Schools encourage teachers and principals to be practical and idealistic simultaneously. The image of a school where all children of all families learn well pushes and pulls the process of inquiry beyond prescribed problem solving by raising unseasonable questions about equality that lack expected answers. In short, then, Equality Schools grow best from the productive tension between theory and practice, the ideal and the real. They are a work in progress owned by the people closest to the learners, not a recipe teachers and principals are to be laboriously trained to imitate and implement. When educators begin to question together how to help all their children learn at high levels of accomplishment, they are continuing the vital American experiment of creating schools worthy of a democracy, public schools of equality.

Notes

1. The following schools have been recognized by the National Coalition for Equality in Learning as Equality Schools: Casey Middle School, Nederland, Ryan, and Washington Bilingual Schools (Boulder Valley, Colorado); Pintlala Elementary School, Catoma Elementary School (Montgomery, Alabama); McDonogh 15 Elementary School (New Orleans, Louisiana); Plymouth Elementary School (Plymouth Meeting, Pennsylvania); Bammel, Beneke, Hirsch, Jenkins, Link, Ponderosa, Salyers, Smith, Twin Creeks,

Winship, and Wunsche Schools (Spring, Texas); and the Juan Linn Math and Science Magnet School (Victoria, Texas).

2. In a major national study, Goodlad (1981) documents the significant discrepancies in curriculum and pedagogy between high and low tracks in public schools.

References

Adler, M. J. (1982). *The Paideia proposal: An educational manifesto.* New York: Macmillan.

Callahan, R. E. (1962). *Education and the cult of efficiency: A study of the social forces that have shaped the administration of the public schools.* Chicago: University of Chicago Press.

Goodlad, J. I. (1963). *The nongraded elementary school.* New York: Harcourt Brace Jovanovich.

Goodlad, J. I. (1981). *A place called school.* New York: McGraw-Hill.

Levin, H. M. (1987). Accelerated schools for the disadvantaged. *Teacher Education Quarterly, 14,* 19-21.

Sizer, T. (1992). *Horace's school: Redesigning the American high school.* Boston: Houghton Mifflin.

Soder, R. (1996). *Democracy, education, and the schools.* San Francisco: Jossey-Bass.

Evaluation in Service of Learning 7

WARD J. GHORY
ROBERT L. SINCLAIR

Thoughtful and resourceful teachers and principals create many effective ways to evaluate the progress children are making in their learning. In individual classrooms and schools, educators find that results from these local evaluations may be used to craft learning conditions that help young people realize their academic promise. In fact, these homemade evaluations are proving to be crucial for ensuring that all children of all families learn well in school. Tailor-made evaluations provide evidence of progress particular students are making in their school learning. Such evaluation results give teachers useful information for guiding decisions that alter the conditions for learning so that the strengths of individuals are used to eliminate their prevailing weaknesses. By looking in detail at how well young people are learning, teachers can make changes in the environment that are likely to result in increased learning.

Yet, what educators discover about the progress of children seldom reaches members of the community, whose judgments about the success of their schools are based largely on external evaluations dominated by the results of standardized tests. Unfortunately, the data gleaned from these tests are often unrelated to the actual work of children and teachers in local schools. Given the emphasis placed by politicians, newspaper editors, television broadcasters, and boards of education on the results of standardized tests, it is little wonder that school leaders become preoccupied with initiatives to raise test scores. But because these tests are usually written at a distance from schools and often do not center on what is being taught or what children are currently learning, test results are not especially revealing. When scores on standardized tests serve as the only primary indicators of success, educators lack sufficient information to help children increase their learning and the public remains uncertain whether schools are actually doing the job they are expected to do. Perhaps it is time to seek a better balance between external tests and local evaluations so that teachers and parents may better determine how well their children are learning and members of the community may become more confident about the effectiveness of their schools.

In this chapter, we explore ways that evaluation and learning are related. First, we underscore the importance of using evaluation to enhance desired learning. Second, we propose a view of evaluation that is anchored to key principles that spring from our work in diverse public schools across the United States. These principles place evaluation in service of learning. Third, we describe some major challenges that educators experience as they improve their capacity to conduct local evaluations.

Connecting Evaluation to Student Learning

We are refining a productive way to guide local schools in determining the effectiveness of their own efforts to increase learning, particularly for those youngsters who live in adverse circumstances and for various reasons are not benefiting from their school experiences. This is being done without relying primarily on externally developed, standard evaluation. Rather, each school reports evidence of progress toward locally defined priorities for student learning. Evidence of community and family support in accomplishing these learning priorities is also collected. Over time, it is possible for educators in local schools to evaluate their own progress. They can indeed master the complicated process of developing evaluation approaches that provide powerful data for wise decisions to improve learning. We have seen, however, that ways of evaluating are closely linked to views about learning. Sadly, we are finding that evaluation is usually connected to a seriously limited view of learning—namely, conditioning. Let us look specifically at the connections between conditioning and standardized tests as a way to determine progress in student learning.

An evaluation relying on standardized tests that emphasize only accurate recall of previously provided information under timed circumstances is closely linked with a view that emphasizes learning as conditioning. Knowledge is treated as relatively static, and learners are conditioned to become pleased and satisfied when expected connections are made between a test question stimulus and a single desired response that is considered correct. The student's behavior becomes motivated by external rewards and punishments in the form of grades and other incentives. Evaluation, then, becomes part of a system of classroom management that controls student behavior in a relatively narrow manner.

When evaluation is based on test performance emphasizing information recognition and retrieval, it may promote overdependence on single sources of information, such as one textbook, and overreliance on single sources of authority, such as only the teacher. Speed of mental processing is overvalued in this evaluation approach. Rate of learning is considered a predictor of intelligence. Those who work best swiftly, autonomously, and silently come out ahead, as do those familiar with the information being tested from previous exposure to it in their homes and cultural context. Students favored by this approach to evaluation and view of learning are considered smart and often receive preferred access to enriched learning environments (similar to a frequent flyer being upgraded to a seat in first class). Students who do not fare well on evaluations that echo conditioning are often, paradoxically, subjected to classroom environments with intensified drill and practice regimes emphasizing information recall (similar to a novice traveler being put on a waiting list for the next flight).

Using the standard approach to evaluation, convergent thinking becomes overvalued and divergent thinking goes begging. We are discovering that when this approach to evaluation is used by default as the primary means for assessing student learning, the result is that standardized tests hinder many youngsters from realizing their academic promise.

Contrasting Approaches to Evaluation and Learning

Educators who are concerned about reaching and teaching all children tend to place evaluation in service of learning. They start with an understanding of their students' strengths and weaknesses and a view about how learning takes place. Their thinking about learning influences the way they evaluate the progress of their students. For example, educators using a multiple intelligence approach to learning recognize that learners differ in their aptitudes (Gardner, 1983). Verbal, visual, spatial, interpersonal, kinesthetic, musical, and mathematical differences in student strengths are expected and accepted. Human variability demands alternatives and educators with this view naturally expect their students to demonstrate what they learn in a variety of ways. Performance is often assessed by a team of teachers who bring a variety of interests to the evaluation task. Students in the learning group may write, construct, debate, draw, measure, or perform as ways of showing what they are learning. As Paul Torrance (1963) demonstrated in his studies of gifted children, when evaluation is changed from an emphasis only on recall of information to consideration of multiple criteria for assessing learning progress, many of the "average" students take over leadership roles and many of the "superior" students realize there are important skills they need to develop. Evaluation based on multiple intelligence describes the strengths and illuminates the needs of learners instead of sorting students by grading and ranking them against each other. An evaluation that results from recognizing individual differences often suggests new directions for creating conditions to promote learning for all students at higher levels of accomplishment.

Homemade evaluations provide teachers with specific information about the progress of individual students to accomplish a desired end in learning. With this information, teachers may create new conditions for learning that are more likely to help students succeed. Also, new ends may be created to match insights about what is needed for individuals to overcome deficiencies in their learning. Because the teacher working with homemade evaluations has data about how individuals are progressing in their learning, it is possible to make decisions that encourage independent learning—learning motivated by the student rather than by an external system of reward and punishment.

We are discovering in our work across the country that successful teachers and effective principals view learning as the practice of "independent problem solving." They value self-directed learning over conditioning. These educators encourage students to construct their own views of knowledge, to define personally meaningful questions, and to develop creative responses to problems they uncover. Evaluation associated with this view of learning shifts toward encouraging students to become involved in defining criteria that may be used to determine whether they have learned well. This view of learning suggests that students should be evaluated in their use of what they have learned. They should demonstrate recently developed skills and knowledge in a setting that is different from where their learning was originally acquired. Evaluation thus opens the door to using learning to tackle real-world problems alive in the community. This emphasis on self-directed learning leads to evaluation centered on application and transfer of learning. The premium is placed on assessing the quality of student problem-solving skills, not on their production of a previously determined "correct" answer. In other words, evaluation gives students an opportunity to use what they have learned to learn something new.

When promoting independent learning, it is important to remember that individuals learn, groups do not. Homemade evaluations center on the progress of individual students, revealing particularities and peculiarities of their minds at work. In contrast, standardized tests usually provide data about the progress of individuals in relation to other students, not in relation to the substance of what they are trying to learn. Seldom do teachers consider individual student performance on specific questions from a standardized test to decide changes in the environment that will help individuals improve their learning. For this reason, the results of homemade evaluations are usually more useful than standardized test data for supporting the practice of independent problem solving.

Changing the Focus for Evaluation

Linking evaluation to views of learning, we come to appreciate how deeply rooted evaluation based on conditioning is in the idea that only what is inside the learner contributes to poor achievement. Too often, evaluation results are interpreted to suggest that low scores are the result of deficiencies in the human condition of the child. The conditions of the school environment are seldom considered as a reason for failure. Rather, failing test grades on narrowly constructed evaluation measures are considered proof positive that a child has not tried or else lacks the capacity to learn well. To question the evaluation—or the view of learning it reflects—is an uncomfortable challenge to most teachers and principals.

Taken to an extreme, evaluations resulting from state competency exams and standardized college placement tests tend to support the practice of sorting young people to determine who will gain access to high-quality learning experiences. Such measures preserve thoughts about learning as conditioning and perpetuate perceptions about evaluation as external reward and punishment. Evaluation is used to *prove* that some students are superior and that most do not have what it takes. Because this evaluation is geared to comparing test results of individuals to the scores of others, it provides little information that would suggest helpful alterations in the learning environment that might *improve* learning for those having difficulty. With standard evaluations centered on conditioning, individuals win, lose, or coast along, as the results distract attention from needed changes in the learning environment while seeming to sort students objectively according to the "intelligence" of those tested. We suggest that until evaluation is placed in service of improving learning and removed from the context of ranking and sorting children, the prevailing evaluation system that persists across our country must be considered a serious impediment to lasting school reform.

A Constructive View of School Evaluation

With colleagues across the United States, we are now refining principles that place improved evaluation in service of increased learning. Educators and community members at the school and district levels are being challenged to consider and adapt these principles to their local circumstances. The principles serve as guides to decision making for evaluation that will help all youngsters succeed in school. For educators accustomed to reliance on externally developed forms of evaluation, the challenge is particularly keen to develop an "ethics of evaluation" that is consistent with self-directed learning and the mission of public education in a democratic society. These principles are intended to help educators confront the misuses of evaluation to sort and rank students. The principles encourage constructive thinking about evaluation as a powerful means for promoting greater excellence and equality in learning.[1]

Teachers, principals, and parents should set learning priorities for local schools based on the specific problems in learning that face students in their particular school and community. Probably, the most enduring legacy of our work is its success in encouraging educators to identify and solve problems interfering with student learning. When we began in 1990, most school faculties did not set priorities; their central offices and school boards did. Faculties were often concerned about the degree to which they were or were not united on a social level—harmonious and supportive, or divided into factions. Moreover, they seldom engaged in the sometimes contentious process of facing, analyzing, and solving the most serious learning problems of their students. Given the opportunity and encouragement, however, local educators learned relatively quickly (in 2 to 3 years) to become more sophisticated in setting and reaching their school priorities.[2] The culture of the school can be carefully crafted to ensure constructive thought and effective action for increasing student learning.

In brief, the problem-solving process we created asks members of the school community to discuss concerns they have about students' learning and to determine a manageable number of priorities for increasing learning during the current school year. The schools form teams of teachers and community resource people to inquire into conditions contributing to learning problems. These study teams then design, implement, and evaluate solutions to identified problems (Smith, 1996). This process contrasts dramatically with the top-down, "one-size-fits-all" approach generally followed, in which all schools in a district address the same problems in the same way, often by using a packaged curriculum or slick staff development program introduced from the outside with a catchy slogan. Simple "shake-and-bake" solutions to complex learning problems provide a false sense of efficiency and prove to be ineffective. If you start with a solution, you are likely considering the wrong problem. As Ralph Tyler (1992) has advised, "Serious problems in school learning cannot be understood or solved on the basis of abstract generalizations or by emulating the analyses and solutions proposed by others. . . . A careful study of each particular case can provide sufficient understanding of the problem to devise an effective solution" (p. 7). The first principle of constructive evaluation, then, is to define the priorities to be accomplished in terms of desired student learning.

Each school staff needs to increase its capacity to evaluate progress toward the learning priorities it has set. We find that school staffs can muster the capacity to evaluate the progress of their own efforts to improve learning. This is a promising finding because one source of confusion about the effectiveness of schools is the inability of local educators to convince the public that they are achieving meaningful results. Without clear-eyed analysis of progress children are making in their learning, educators tend to perpetuate the existing school culture and maintain current curriculum. They cannot accurately assess whether progress is being made without determining desired outcomes for learning. By setting priorities for learning, creating and implementing solutions, and accurately charting their progress, educators can internalize an ongoing improvement process. Simply put, the capacity to evaluate in the local schools makes it possible for educators to create conditions for effective learning and to report their accomplishments to the public.

Also, we find that the local capacity for evaluation is an important variable for assessing and building organizational strength. Schools where the internal capacity for evaluation is lacking remain overreliant on external measures of success. In these schools, teachers are suspicious of evaluation because they see it as a tool of power exercised by the central administration, the board of education, or the state to prove that their work is lacking. Evaluation is not viewed as a resource that provides useful information for guiding teachers' decision making about changes they want to make to improve their own school environment. The reliance on external evaluations seems to lead to an overemphasis on "beating" the pressure generated by standardized tests. This distorts the school program in the direction of test preparation, isolation of students identified as excellent or poor test takers, and remedial tutoring strategies based on narrow rewards and punishments common to conditioned learning. By contrast, educators in schools that grow more able to evaluate their own effectiveness can use results to guide instruction, change curriculum, and communicate with parents about priorities and progress in their children's learning. The educators become increasingly self-reliant and gain greater leeway in setting policies to determine their own destiny because the rationale behind their actions is to improve learning of all children of all families.

Evaluation must be closely tied to desired learning. Our collaboration with educators in schools across the country suggests that evaluation should be clearly linked to what is being taught. We should not evaluate what we do not teach. As every schoolchild knows, it simply is not "fair" to be evaluated on objectives that are not taught or to be kept in the dark about the subject matter being evaluated. For school leaders, too, there is little benefit to receive evaluation results about accomplishments of knowledge, attitudes, or skills that have not been taught to students. Unfortunately, this is what usually happens when evaluations use results from tests that follow the convenient myth of universal coverage of content at set grade levels. This procrustean thinking produces inaccurate evidence about learning that encourages misguided changes in the school environment. Simply put, we must have thoughtful ways to determine what our students are achieving and need to learn, creative environments that help them succeed, and constructive approaches to evaluate what has actually been accomplished.

Evaluation should serve learning. This principle of evaluation suggests that results help us consider the extent to which students are accomplishing desired learning and the changes in curriculum and instruction that may foster even more effective learning, particularly for students on the margins of school life who are not succeeding. Hence, if questions on tests determine what is taught, the process is backward.[3] Evaluation should help us determine what is being accomplished rather than dictating what should be learned. We evaluate to improve learning, not to prove that some students know what is on a test. For example, evaluation may help promote the transfer of learning to new experiences by encouraging students to apply their knowledge and skills to novel settings related in discernible ways to the context in which students were originally taught. Evaluation should not be a post mortem for learning but a continuation of learning.

Done well, evaluation can also foster learning by helping students gain a deeper understanding of why the objectives they are trying to accomplish are important to their lives. Insights into the ends of learning may lead students to devise their own ways for determining the progress they are making toward meeting these ends. Awareness of the purpose and potential uses of evaluation creates greater commitment and motivation on the part of learners to take evaluation seriously and to do their best work. One reason some students perform poorly on tests is that they distrust the whole process and refuse to invest themselves in what seems to be a game stacked against their succeeding. Informed students, who see evaluation as a credible and fair extension of the learning process, will also, no doubt, raise critical questions likely to sharpen and improve the evaluation approach, if heeded. This suggests that evaluation linked to learning may make the entire approach more inclusive of students. If it is not clear how the results of evaluation will be used to help students learn, the evaluation should not take place.

Students should be provided with a variety of realistic situations to demonstrate what they have learned. We find that students desire realistic situations in which they can demonstrate what they are accomplishing. Learning should be evaluated where it is used, not where it is acquired. Science fairs to show creative thinking, debates to exercise reasoning, community service projects to help older people with chores, art shows to display creative talent, letters to congressional representatives requesting changes in laws— these are familiar situations for assessing whether learning is being accomplished. Because students understand new information and express themselves best through a variety of situations, they should be evaluated using a variety of ways to observe their behavior closely. Overreliance on any single means of collecting data for evaluation (tests, essays, performances, exhibitions, portfolios, tutorials, class participation, and so on) unfairly favors some students over others and may miss the progress made by those less able to demonstrate what they know in the preferred manner. Similarly, when student work is viewed by a number of observers in addition to the teacher, learners benefit by seeing their accomplishments reflected from many perspectives.

Evaluation must be more than looking for accurate recall of previous learning. Through the evaluation experience, students must be challenged to succeed with difficult tasks that motivate them to excel but do not discourage them from trying. Frequently, this constructive challenge occurs when they are asked to solve new problems by using previous learning. In this way, knowledge and insight are expanded by the evaluation process, not merely confirmed by being graded as "correct" or "wrong." It seems reasonable to conclude that a multifaceted approach to evaluation is one that makes sense given the diversity of academic strengths and weaknesses of young people and the complicated nature of determining whether individuals are learning what the school is teaching. There is no one best way to learn, and there is no one best way to evaluate. Human variability demands alternatives.

Evaluation results should be used to improve learning. The major constructive purpose of evaluation, then, is to improve learning, not to prove that a specific program works well or poorly, that students of a particular group perform better or worse than others, or that one student is smarter than another. Successful evaluation holds up a well-lit, carefully focused mirror that allows teachers, students, and parents to identify and understand conditions that hinder or foster learning. Evaluation can be designed to create a clear picture of unique individual characteristics and detailed aspects of their settings to help explain how particular students learn best and why they make errors. A careful examination of evaluation results should provide a deeper understanding of what needs to be done to improve conditions in school and at home so that learning will increase.

To aid learning, evaluation results need to be stated in simple, crisp language. Too often, abstract statistics and technical jargon conceal useful information. This leaves students—and their parents and teachers—mystified about what they actually did wrong or right, fostering a sense of helplessness and ineptitude. By explaining incomplete learning with fuzzy results, educators fall back, somewhat defensively, on inalterable variables like parent income, family structure, or years of education as reasons for failure. When powerful or even simple statistical techniques are not used judiciously or explained clearly, they severely reduce the depth of a learner's experience and accomplishments to shallow numerical scores. Again, the purpose of evaluation is to understand better the progress students are making in their learning and the conditions that help or hinder their accomplishments. The intent is not to present a complex psychometric analysis that is silent and neutral about directions for improvement. Results of evaluation should be reported in ways that are understood by those being evaluated.

The five principles we propose for evaluation have accrued an ethical dimension that guides decision making about how evaluation will be conducted and how results will be used to improve learning. Developing a constructive way of thinking about evaluation is a complicated venture because past evaluation practices are deeply embedded in the ongoing culture of the school. Because evaluation is also closely tied to how success and failure of schools and students are presented to the public, the stakes are high when any changes in how we evaluate are attempted. The purpose and practice of evaluation must be raised as urgent ethical issues before evaluation can reclaim a more central place in school reform and before school reform can make a lasting difference in the learning of young people.

Creating a Capacity for Evaluation in the Local School

In our work across the country, we see teachers and principals finding precious little time to evaluate how effective their school is in helping all children succeed in their learning. Too often, the educators do not know how to go about designing or conducting an evaluation. It is not clear if their difficulty in determining the progress in children's learning comes from a shortage in skill, a lack of interest, or an unwillingness to take on yet another responsibility. The hesitation of local educators to evaluate, however, does not justify relying solely on external evaluations driven by standardized tests as a means for determining school effectiveness. We are discovering that with careful nurturing and innovative leadership development, school staffs can indeed gain a capacity for evaluating their own effectiveness. Teachers and principals do see that evaluation is a key to unlocking the problems that hinder too many young people from succeeding in school. Once professional educators are convinced that they have the responsibility and authority to evaluate their school, they find the time, develop the skills, and take the lead for determining how well their children learn what the school is expected to teach.

It is important to avoid advancing a single model for improving evaluation to be implemented in every school. Instead of seeking one facile solution, we suggest educators start by facing practical challenges that promote spirited dialogue and encourage thoughtful decisions. Simply put, we trust each school faculty to act as a community of scholars who tackle these challenges and make their own plans for constructive evaluation. Because there is no set model, there is no single path to blaze so schools may improve their capacity to evaluate their own progress. We find, however, four persistent challenges that must be considered for meaningful evaluation to take place in local schools.

Setting Priorities for Learning

The first challenge is to set priorities closely tied to learning problems experienced by children in the local community. We find that the problems considered crucial by school staffs change as the faculty becomes more sophisticated with the process of teacher decision making and more thoughtful about the impact of the school environment on student learning. First attempts at selecting learning priorities tend to focus on student deficiencies—poor attendance, low test scores, weak study habits, disruptive behavior. There is precious little evidence to support the existence of a learning problem. Hence, it is difficult to set priorities. The solutions first identified are standard ones that intensify current conditions—stricter discipline, increased accountability, additional remedial training, and greater use of mentors. Gradually, a constructive view of student assets emerges. Teachers start to believe that the conditions necessary for student success can be created in each school by redesigning the learning environment rather than by forcing students to fit into the prevailing environment. Accordingly, faculty set priorities that change the way teaching occurs or that lead to more responsive curriculum. Teachers and principals also try to improve themselves to be effective with students who are not benefiting from their school experiences.

Determining if Students Are Learning

In the hurly-burly of school life, it is not easy to determine what quantitative and qualitative information will directly indicate whether specific learning is being accomplished. This is the second challenge. When teachers try to see whether students are learning better, they often state priorities in terms of means concerning adult behaviors, working conditions, instructional techniques, or curriculum materials. There is a preoccupation with means. With time, priorities emphasize ends rather than means. Less attention is directed to gimmicky teaching strategies and more attention is given to learning outcomes students will accomplish. Replacing priorities based on means with priorities aiming for desired ends sets the stage for useful evaluation of student learning.

Creating an Evaluation Design

Another challenge is to build an evaluation design that has the backing of teachers and principals in the local school. The most successful evaluations result when the staff invests time in creating a careful design. Educators in Spring, Texas, for example, settled on a flexible protocol for evaluation. In Spring schools, after a learning problem was identified, study teams checked test results, compared findings with other schools, and interviewed students and parents to confirm the existence of the problem and to make sure it was a truly important one to confront. Once the planned intervention was in place, study teams took time to confirm that problem-solving actions actually occurred. Next, they measured changes in student behavior against a specified standard by comparing selected results to the initial status of the learners served. They also looked for unintended effects, positive or negative, and for alternate reasons for changes in outcomes (Smith, 1996). Evaluation conducted in this manner encourages teachers and principals to take a searching look at their efforts to improve learning. Developing an evaluation design for a local school ensures a connection between what is being evaluated and what the school is helping children learn.

Collecting Data

As most external evaluations cannot possibly address the specific learning problems targeted by professional educators in each school, another evaluation challenge is to find or develop useful data collection tools that center on the specific learning problems. Local school staffs take over responsibility for data collection in three ways. First, they make selective use of test and survey data already being collected by the district or state. Often, it proves discouraging to track achievement this way, not only because the learning being measured may bear little relation to what is being taught at school, but also because students tested in one year are not tested the following year. This makes it difficult to determine the progress of individual students over time.

Second, teachers find and administer evaluation instruments that relate directly to their school priorities. For example, in Boulder

Valley, Colorado, where educators in a number of schools sought to improve the responsiveness of their programs to the diversity of their students, the Ramirez Cultural Diversity Inventory was administered in consecutive years to track progress.

A third approach to collecting data is to develop locally the instruments needed to determine student progress toward accomplishing learning priorities. For example, staff at Apple Valley High School in Minnesota developed the concept of the Graduation Achievement Rate (GAR) for identifying students who were considered academically marginal because they were not making adequate progress to graduate on time. The GAR was expressed as a percentage and determined by dividing the total number of credits earned by the total number of credits expected. This method was used to identify students who for various reasons were not moving toward graduation. This led to accurate record keeping to highlight the school's progress with these students.

A powerful force for school improvement, then, is created when faculty set priorities, try new approaches, and determine whether they are succeeding in fostering better learning. Promoting such inquiry into student learning is a promising way to make evaluation more central in the process of school renewal. Leaders in schools and school districts must face the troubling contradictions of evaluation that works best with only some of our learners while blocking many from realizing their full promise. The solutions to the problems experienced by learners lie in the hands of the people who know their strengths and weaknesses. By creating a local capacity for evaluation, we place a practical, powerful tool for improvement in the hands of the professional educators who are closest to the children the local school is expected to serve.

Closing

The best evaluation describing a school's quality to its own community probably consists of a blend of externally generated and locally developed forms of evaluation. Data about learning presented by standardized tests or by attendance and discipline reports still hold a place in the portfolio of information that helps us judge the progress of students and the effectiveness of a school. Yet, we must be far more critical of the limitations of these data, more aware of the biases, inaccuracies, and inconsistencies those easy numbers mask, if they are to play an appropriate role in presenting a true picture of a school and the young people who learn there.

In this chapter, we call for evaluation that serves learning by shining light on the environment where learning takes place and illuminating the accomplishments of individual students. Evaluation should provide data for ongoing improvement, practical information the people inside a school can use to change the conditions under which their students perform. In our democratic system emphasizing local control of education, the public deserves to know what learning priorities the teachers and principal of each particular school are helping students accomplish. The public will want to find out what educators are doing to reach these priorities and what progress they are making.

External evaluations, especially those reliant on standardized tests, are not up to this challenge. By placing so much emphasis on their supposedly objective measurements of what children know, external evaluations are opaque about the context for learning and silent about needed steps for improvement. Overreliance on this approach to evaluation too often leaves the public disconnected from the learning initiatives that take place and critical of the students and schools.

External evaluations need to be balanced and tempered with local school evaluations. These homemade approaches reveal learning in the reality of particular classrooms and schools. Local evaluations give parents insight into educational programs and appreciation of individual accomplishments. In turn, this seems to develop the pride and commitment that leads a community to grade its own schools higher than other schools across the country. Local evaluations also suggest directions teachers and concerned parents may take for ongoing improvement in the schools they care for. In our work with schools, we find that an improved sense of identification with public schools and a renewed commitment to their mission result from sharing the educational vision of local schools and the progress of all children with those who live and work in their neighborhoods. Schools can and should tell their educational story in a more compelling way than any test scores listed in the morning paper can convey. By restoring evaluation in the public eye through a thoughtful combination of externally generated and locally developed approaches, we will make evaluation an integral part of all children learning well.

Notes

1. These principles were described in Ghory (1996, pp. 92-93). For an earlier conception, see Ghory and Sinclair (1994).

2. By the third year of the project, 93% of the schools were reporting priorities; in Years 4 and 5, 100% of the member schools set and reported priorities. Further analysis of the priority setting process is available in the Annual Reports of the National Coalition for Equality in Learning.

3. In the National Coalition, we hold that decision making about curriculum should be in the hands of those closest to the learner, the teachers and parents in the local community who know best what the children do well and what hinders them in their learning.

References

Gardner, H. (1983). *Frames of mind.* New York: Basic Books.

Ghory, W. J. (1996, April). Reclaiming evaluation: The Cinderella of school reform. *Equity & Excellence in Education, 29*(1), 92-93.

Ghory, W. J., & Sinclair, R. L. (1994, April). *Improving evaluation of student learning.* Paper presented at the Annual Meeting of the American Educational Research Association, New Orleans, LA.

Smith, R. G. (1996, April). Fashioning effective solutions: The promise of school study teams. *Equity & Excellence in Education, 29*(1), 20-29.

Torrance, P. E. (1963). *Gifted children in the classroom.* New York: Macmillan.

Tyler, R. W. (1992) *Improving school effectiveness.* Amherst, MA: National Coalition for Equality in Learning.

8 Leadership for Learning

ROBERT L. SINCLAIR

WARD J. GHORY

In previous chapters, educators participating in the National Coalition for Equality in Learning described and explained the progress and problems of this experiment to improve the learning of children in public schools. Also, the chapters included reflections on what was learned over the years about changing educational practice. Simply stated, this book reports the lessons learned by professional educators from various corners of the enterprise who work daily to reach and teach all children of all families, including those young people floating on the margins of school life and at risk of failing to realize the promise of their potential.

The reader can tease out innovative thinking intended to guide creative leadership and discern possible actions that may help local schools become even more effective places for high-quality learning on equal terms. The schools and people who joined together in this national effort to increase learning by improving schools represent a microcosm of problems, practices, and promises existing in public schools across the United States. Hence, what can be gleaned from efforts of the National Coalition for Equality in Learning may catch the imagination of leaders who realize the importance of making public education a more powerful means for equality in our contemporary democratic society.

In this chapter, we distill a set of constructive directions for leadership that we hope will improve public schools in a manner respectful of their crucial mission in a successful democracy.

Directions for Leadership

Let us start with the position that public schools are responsible for helping all children of all families learn well. This is the promise of schools in a democracy: that every young person—regardless of cultural background, economic status, skin color, or tested ability—will develop academic competencies and social skills needed for a productive and fulfilling life. Our fundamental challenge as teachers, administrators, parents, and community members is to ensure that our schools live up to this responsibility. Leaders may want to remind the public that we will not realize our potential as a nation until we judge the success of our schools by how well everyone in them succeeds.

Our schools need leaders who focus on promoting learning more than on managing schools. Changing how our schools are organized, governed, or funded will not necessarily alter how educators think about ideas or interact with one another. It is a simple fact that programs and policies do not improve learning; people willing to identify and solve problems improve learning. No, we do not need more management; we need more imagination and inspiration, more personal insight and initiative. This suggests that it may be useful for leaders to initiate conversations and foster actions in their local schools and communities to identify the strengths and weaknesses of students. By helping teachers and parents better understand the problems students experience in their learning, it is possible to determine priorities for improving learning. With clear ends in mind, educational leaders must concentrate on creating intellectual, social, and physical conditions likely to encourage learning for all children.

Leaders focused on learning encourage us to change the way we think and act. They derive their satisfaction and joy from contributing to improvements in school cultures that will enable even more students and teachers to do their best work. We need leaders who help us realize that failure and frustration in the classroom or in the community are not reasons to doubt our abilities but occasions to strengthen our resolve. Such supportive leadership may come from many different people in many different ways as teachers, principals, parents, and staff unite behind priorities they have chosen for improving the learning of all children. In school after school, we have found that if problems are approached analytically, they can be attacked successfully. Leaders need to help others realize that it is not necessary to find one master solution to all learning problems. Rather, it is more productive to thoughtfully pick a few compelling problems blocking the learning of their children and get started on creating and trying out practical solutions.

In this book, we equate school improvement with solving problems students have in their learning. It is important to consider that necessary and enduring improvements must come from within local schools, not from state houses or the White House. Packaged curricula or prescribed teaching methods developed outside the school and imposed on local educators seldom fit the specific needs of students experiencing difficulty learning. What worked in one school may not work in every school. Nor will intensifying current conditions make the difference we need. Instead, more students will learn well when teachers and others most familiar with student strengths and difficulties work carefully to understand unique problems in learning. Educators and parents in local schools have to exercise their creative intelligence to solve the most important learning problems facing their children. No one outside the school can do this as well as they can. Teachers should be encouraged to be active decision makers because they are closest to students and have the most information about the strengths and difficulties students experience in their learning. Encouraging teachers to make wise decisions about student learning is another direction for effective leadership.

As explained in this book, the most meaningful understanding of student learning emerges when educators join in a carefully considered process of collaborative inquiry aimed at discovering learning problems, designing and testing optional solutions, and assessing the progress of students. The authors in this book explain the effective operation of study teams as a means for using the strengths of individual students and teachers to overcome barriers to productive learning. Through collaboration, teachers realize that they are not only permitted to act on their own intellectual initiative but expected to do so. Stimulated by one another to think creatively and carefully, teachers soon see there is no one way to help children improve their learning. The wise direction for action is to initiate ways to solve problems rather than wait for answers ready-made.

To help children from diverse backgrounds, including those living and learning in adverse circumstances and those plagued by the complications of affluence, meet the complex challenges they face, leaders must act on their understanding that significant learning takes place in settings outside school as well as in school. Too often, educators, parents, and community leaders operate separately, without listening to one another's stories, without trying to find out how the problems one group sees actually look from another perspective. If schools are going to help more students achieve at higher levels of accomplishment, there has to be a combined effort among schools, families, and youth-serving agencies. Leaders of schools assist families to increase their contributions to the learning of their children, just as families can help schools reform so that they reach and teach all children. By creating and combining conditions in school and nonschool settings, increased learning may be promoted for all youngsters, including those who are falling into the cracks of our educational system. This is a pragmatic direction to create conditions for effective learning that leaders should consider.

Educators in local schools are likely to claim the process of their own improvement when they develop greater internal capacity to evaluate the progress being made toward accomplishing the priorities they have set. Evaluation, too, has to be placed in service of improving learning. This is a crucial direction for action that demands thoughtful leadership. Too often, educators, parents, and community members permit scores on standardized tests to serve as the primary measure of the quality of their schools. They accommodate themselves to the tyranny of external evaluations that mainly are employed to compare students against one another so that they can be sorted for differential access to enriched learning environments. By creating and using homemade evaluations, local educators can gather information about how their own students are learning what they are trying to teach. The results of these evaluations may be used to craft learning conditions that help even more young people succeed in school. An essential part of solving learning problems is to look in detail at what progress young people make and then change the environment in ways that are likely to result in increased learning. Another direction for leadership is to blend the results of external evaluations with the findings of local evaluations to achieve a clear picture of student progress. Local educators can then report to their immediate communities the current quality of their schools, request assistance for improvement, and celebrate excellent accomplishments.

In brief, we advocate a school improvement process that stresses the importance of equality by insisting that all children succeed in their learning. Just as we emphasize that teachers practice creative intelligence in local schools as a constructive path to taking the lead in helping children solve their learning problems, we also advocate that youngsters become self-directed learners who do not depend on external rewards and punishments associated with learning by conditioning. In the schools we are developing, students are encouraged to practice intellectual independence so that they are prepared to participate constructively in our democracy and avoid the intellectual subservience that tragically handicaps those who have not been well educated. A basic message of this book is to suggest that any effective approach to school improvement must be consistent with democratic values of striving for equality, respect for individuals, pragmatic problem solving, and local decision making. We believe that the best hope for significant and lasting renewal of public schools is to restore their place of importance in our contemporary democratic society. This is a leadership direction for school improvement that demands creative leaders who understand the role of public schools in a democracy.

This book suggests that the last and first obligation of educators in each local school, as it mirrors the democratic society it serves, is to take the lead in improving conditions for learning so that all children may realize the promise of their potential in their lifetime. The ideas advanced and challenges presented in this book remind educators that the public school is the instrument society has created for ensuring that the opportunity to obtain a high-quality education is made available to all children of all families on equal terms. In fact, the public school is the only institution with the responsibility of aiding all children in their learning, no matter what conditions prevail in their homes or what circumstances dominate in their lives. Some schools are effective at meeting this obligation, but many are not.

Unfortunately, too many youngsters are not benefiting fully from their school experiences. These children, who tend to come from poor homes, disconnect from the conditions designed to help them learn and are forced to the margins of school life where they do not gain equal access to opportunities for effective learning. This book suggests that committed teachers and caring family members working together can assist some children in overcoming such experiences of inequality by converting unequal treatment into a motivating force for achieving excellence. Yet, the perception of being treated as less lingers for others and hinders their accomplishments. Local schools and their surrounding communities must be encouraged to attack this persistent problem. The resolution of this problem demands creative leaders who have the skill to help children on the margins improve their learning.

The progress described in this book shows that it is possible to rekindle the desire of educators to reach and teach all children, even those who for various reasons do not seem to fit and are at risk of failing. Reaching and teaching these marginal students even more effectively is not charitable social work; it is the centerpiece of this nation's educational mission. Our work with educators across the country is intended to attack this stubborn problem of marginality so that equality in public schools is increased.

We conclude this chapter by sharing what we are learning about the problem of marginality that persists in too many schools. This problem keeps rearing its head and it must be addressed if public schools are to help all young people learn well. We are discovering that forming learning communities in local schools is a promising way to reach marginal students. By sharing ideas about marginality and community, we hope to encourage immediate and sustained leadership for creating conditions that improve learning and ensure equality in public schools. It is helpful for leaders to gain insight into marginality and community because resulting actions on these inter-related issues are likely to provide an opening for significant changes in school practice.

Marginality

We are discovering that marginality occurs when there is a disconnection between students and the conditions designed for their learning. This complex situation arises from many sources and takes many forms. Various types of children become marginal in schools—the youngster not working up to potential, the understimulated exceptional learner, the child with a long history of academic failure, and the one suddenly performing poorly despite previous success. Children may become marginal regardless of gender, ethnic background, family structure, or economic circumstance, although these variables do seem to increase the likelihood of problems with school. Those on the margins of successful learning include children "at risk" from low-income homes as well as troubled youths from well-to-do families. Gifted youngsters can become marginal. Marginal students may live in urban, rural, or suburban locations. For some, the experience of marginality will be short lived. Yet, for many, initial disconnection will be a critical step in developing habits and attitudes making marginality a way of life (for a comprehensive analysis of the marginal student problem in public schools, see Sinclair & Ghory, 1987).

To be "marginal" is to be caught in a *condition* of strained relations with school and persistent struggles with learning. As a result, children on the margins are located in a *position* on the outskirts of the school environment, alienated from the setting designed to promote their learning. Educators often blame the child for this disconnection. But this common approach of blaming the victim fails to account for the role of the environment in influencing behavior. All students are products of family and community settings that predispose them to patterns of behavior that are more or less functional in a particular school environment. The local school typically builds on, refines, or causes reconsideration of these patterns. This means that when a student becomes marginal, it is crucial to consider how the school, family, or community environment may be forcing a disconnection that hinders learning.

It is disturbing to realize that all children may be at risk of becoming at least temporarily disconnected from full and productive involvement in classrooms and schools. To analyze the responsibility of educators for children who do not succeed in school, it is critical to realize that differences in learning result from two-sided interactions between an individual and an environment. To solve problems of marginality, leaders need ways of thinking and acting that hold both ends of the individual-environment equation in balance. Use of the term marginal to explain problems of learning shifts the perspective from deeply seated troubles rooted in individuals to problematic relationships between individuals and school environments. After all, differences between children are not the real problem. Rather, the primary concern is the ability of educators to respond to variations in learning that result from previous and current experiences. If we perceive that individuals alone are responsible for the problems they have in learning, it is easier to cast the responsibility of the educator in distant and benevolent terms. But if we begin to see ways in which school environments tolerate and even promote difficulties that children experience, the responsibilities of educators become more urgent and clear.

Another direction that leaders should consider is to make sure that the conditions in schools do not contribute to problems of marginality. To this end, when children are seen moving to the margins, it is necessary for educators to identify the problems students have in their learning and acknowledge the difficulties schools have in responding to human variability. The marginality of an individual is relative and changeable, a matter of degree. It seems that the degree of marginality depends not only on the actions of the student but also on the way the behavior is viewed and treated by educators. Problematic behaviors are not an individual's total personality or behavioral repertoire; they are responses to how students perceive their environment and how they are being treated. In our work, we find that children on the margins can change even deepseated, unproductive habits, just as constructive changes can be made in relatively static educational environments. As Dewey (1963) emphasized, it is the role of the educator to change conditions until experiences are created that promote learning.

Improvement in conditions for learning, then, will not be accomplished simply by intensifying current features of school environments that are problematic to the very people we hope to assist. Attempts to ease disconnected and uninspired learners into compliance with a more demanding version of the conditions that drove them to the edge in the first place will not suffice. A shift in perspective is needed. School and family settings must become joined so that a more responsible environment for learning may be crafted. In plain terms, a community for learning must be designed to serve marginal students better. This is another constructive direction for school leadership.

Community

Educators working to build communities for learning suggest that a community is a formal or informal group of people who share common views and values, who tolerate a range of differences, and who actively support one another in pursuit of a common end that transcends their individual needs. People in a community believe in something shared. They get together regularly to deepen their commitment and understanding and to develop mutual aspirations. A community for learning, then, may consist of primary relationships among students, teachers, and family members who can help each other accomplish individual and common goals.

Thinking about community reminds us that humans are social beings. We are stimulus seeking, so to be without community often results in loneliness. Life without community, if it persists, may contribute to deviant behavior and personal despair. To live in a large apartment complex and not know anyone is to experience an absence of community. Being at a sporting event and not having any association with others may result in a failure to experience community. Similarly, not understanding one's school assignments or persistently misinterpreting group expectations for acceptable behavior in the classroom may also lead to loss of a sense of community.

We are discovering in our work that children who are marginal often do not have people in their immediate circle who prize academic accomplishments or encourage attitudes and habits that are necessary to be successful in learning what schools are expected to teach. Although all parents want their children to do well in school, many marginal youngsters are socialized to adopt behaviors that conflict with school expectations. They seem to become caught between wanting to do well in school and not wanting to be seen as untrue to the cultural norms learned in the home or the behavior expected in the neighborhood. Marginal students face contradictory pressures without clear direction from significant others who can model and support behavior that leads to school success without loss of personal integrity. Under these circumstances, the creation of a community for learning where none exists shows promise as a means for resolving the alienation that marginal students experience. The community becomes a sanctuary for learning, a welcoming starting point rather than an alienating pressure point.

Our work also shows that some children are skilled at building or joining a community to correct a void in their human interactions and to help them accomplish desired learning. The ability of young people to recognize and seek membership in communities with constructive ends is important. Some communities are dysfunctional. We find, for example, that youths who are severely marginal often seek membership in a community of marginal colleagues whose goals may be opposed to learning in school. This, of course, makes effective intervention extremely difficult. Robert Merton (1938) helps us understand that the more deeply individuals internalize their marginal status, the more powerful the intervention must become.

It is important for leaders to recognize that teachers, parents, and children can develop a powerful community for learning by creating supportive enclaves within a larger environment. For example, parents and teachers can join together to assist their children in obtaining desired skills and competencies. These educative communities start with parents finding common ground with teachers concerned about their children doing well. Again, a promising approach for reaching and teaching all students is the forming of responsive communities for children who struggle with their learning.

Educators involved in our work report that marginal students often are presented with the same school environment as other students, but they become part of a different community or have no community at all. Physical, social, and intellectual conditions in school, then, are not the sole determiners of community. A community is also in the mind, and the perceptions of marginal students decisively influence their behavior. Hence, it is important to discover the image of a student's perceived community so that constructive designing and careful redesigning of the learning environment can take place (Ghory, 1978). This is another direction for leaders to take to change school practice and improve student learning.

Closing

When children fail in their learning, society loses the benefit of educated citizens and individuals lose the opportunity to experience a productive and fulfilling life in our democracy. Educators need to reach and teach these students on the margins of success and help them become productive learners. One crucial challenge that educators must face, then, is to find meaningful and enduring ways to serve children who have not found sufficient reasons or means for academic and personal success available to them in the past. We hope that the directions for leadership and the ideas about marginality and community advanced in this chapter will help educators improve conditions for learning.

It is time for educators to alter the course of reform from the imposition of legislation and policies that demand uniform changes in all schools to the cultivation of priorities and actions that solve particular learning problems in local schools. If considered carefully and implemented wisely, the efforts of the National Coalition for Equality in Learning may help us make this reorientation a practical reality and start a significant improvement in public education—one that will sustain educators as they strive to meet their responsibility for preparing all daughters and all sons of all families for constructive participation in our democracy.

References

Dewey, J. (1963). *Experience and education.* New York: Collier.
Ghory, W. J. (1978). *Alternative educational environments: Marginal learner perceptions of curriculum conditions in public alternative high schools.* Unpublished doctoral dissertation, University of Massachusetts, Amherst.
Merton, R. K. (1938). Social structure and anomie. *American Sociological Review, 3,* 672-682.
Sinclair, R. L., & Ghory, W. J. (1987). *Reaching marginal students: A primary concern for school renewal.* Berkeley, CA: McCutchan.

Index

formal, compared to practical
inquiry, 53-54
teacher. *See* Teacher research
weakness of, 43
Residency status, 26
Resistance to change, 27-28
Resources, allocation of, 86-87, 90
Respect for individuals, 5-6
Restructuring of schools, 26
Robinson, J. L., 23
Rote exercises, limitations of, 16
Rousseau, J.-J., 11

Safety, 19-21, 23
School-family relations:
Equality Schools and, 93
learning from families and, 61-81
See also Families
Schools:
as organizations, 26, 27-28, 48,
107
changing roles of, 78
culture of, 79-80
disconnection from, in
marginality, 123-125
See also Families; Learning;
Public education; Students;
Teachers
Secondary schools:
students as advocates in, 92
study teams in, 52-53
Self-directed learning, 104, 122
Self-education, 70
Self-esteem, 15, 20
Showers, B., 55
Single-parent families, 76, 77
Siskin, L. S., 52
Sizer, T., 85
Social services, 34
ªSocioeconomicº assumptions, 17
Solutions, of problems. *See*
Collaborative inquiry;
Problem solving
Sorting, of students, 105. *See also*
Grouping, of students
Special education services, 91-92

Spirals, and conservation of
insights, 73, 75, 81
Spirit, human. *See* Human spirit
Standardized tests:
conditioning and, 102, 104-105
limitations of, 36-37, 94, 100-101,
114-115
pressure from, 107
State agencies, power transferred
to, 3
Status relations, between families
and school personnel, 75-76
Stories, characteristics of, 62-63. *See
also* Family stories
Structural resistance, to change,
27-28
Students:
as advocates, 92
as individuals, 5-6, 12-13, 39
as individuals, and evaluation,
103, 104
as individuals, and study teams,
44, 46, 50, 51
as individuals, in Equality
Schools, 90-92
capability of all, 88
challenges for all, 90-91
cooperation among, 36
curriculum development by, 35
diversity of, 91, 92-93
evaluation design by, 104, 108-109
evaluation of. *See* Evaluation
expectations for, 15-16, 50-51
feelings of, 14-15
grouping of, 13, 37, 46, 91-92
in Equality Schools, 87-96
labeling of, 6-7, 46, 50-51
language of, 26
marginal, 123-127
self-directed learning by, 104, 122
sorting of, 105
strengths of, 49-50
weaknesses of, 119. *See also*
Problem identification;
Problem solving
See also Learning; Teachers
Study teams, 29-33, 120